Specialist Support Approaches to Autism Spectrum Disorder Students in Mainstream Settings

of related interest

**Career Training and Personal Planning for Students
with Autism Spectrum Disorders**
A Practical Resource for Schools
Vicki Lundine and Catherine Smith
Foreword by Jo-Anne Seip
ISBN-13: 978 1 84310 440 7   ISBN-10: 1 84310 440 7

Autism, Access and Inclusion on the Front Line
Confessions of an Autism Anorak
Matthew Hesmondhalgh
Foreword by Jacqui Jackson
ISBN-13: 978 1 84310 393 6   ISBN-10: 1 84310 393 1

The Complete Guide to Asperger's Syndrome
Tony Attwood
ISBN-13: 978 1 84310 495 7   ISBN-10: 1 84310 495 4

Asperger Syndrome - What Teachers Need to Know
Matt Winter
ISBN-13: 978 1 84310 143 7   ISBN-10: 1 84310 143 2

Nonverbal Learning Disabilities at School
Educating Students with NLD, Asperger Syndrome and Related Conditions
Pamela B. Tanguay
Foreword by Sue Thompson
ISBN-13: 978 1 85302 941 7   ISBN-10: 1 85302 941 6

Incorporating Social Goals in the Classroom
**A Guide for Teachers and Parents of Children with High-Functioning
Autism and Asperger Syndrome**
Rebecca A. Moyes
Foreword by Susan J. Moreno
ISBN-13: 978 1 85302 967 7   ISBN-10: 1 85302 967 X

**Addressing the Challenging Behavior of Children with
High-Functioning Autism/Asperger Syndrome in the Classroom**
A Guide for Teachers and Parents
Rebecca A. Moyes
ISBN-13: 978 1 84310 719 4   ISBN-10: 1 84310 719 8

Specialist Support Approaches to Autism Spectrum Disorder Students in Mainstream Settings

Sally Hewitt

Jessica Kingsley Publishers
London and Philadelphia

First published in 2005
by Jessica Kingsley Publishers
116 Pentonville Road
London N1 9JB, UK
and
400 Market Street, Suite 400
Philadelphia, PA 19106, USA

www.jkp.com

Library of Congress Cataloging in Publication Data
Hewitt, Sally, 1961-
Specialist support approaches to autism spectrum disorder students in mainstream settings / Sally Hewitt.
p. cm.
Includes bibliographical references and index.
ISBN 1-84310-290-0 (pbk.)
1. Autistic children--Education--United States. 2. Inclusive education--United States. I. Title.
LC4718.H49 2005
371.94--dc22

2004014270

British Library Cataloguing in Publication Data
A CIP catalogue record for this book is available from the British Library

ISBN-13: 978 1 84310 290 8
ISBN-10: 1 84310 290 0

Printed and Bound in Great Britain by
Athenaeum Press, Gateshead, Tyne and Wear

He stilled the storm to a whisper; the waves of the sea were hushed. They were glad when it grew calm, and he guided them to their desired haven. (Psalm 107:29–30)

This book is for Shaw

Acknowledgements

With thanks to Julie Crate; Sandra Fisher, Annette Clarke and Sue Sengupta; and the many parents, staff and pupils I've been privileged to work with.

   With special thanks to Sam, Will, Hannah and Lillie; my parents; and Downham Market Christian Fellowship.

Contents

Introduction

Towards inclusive schooling

Mainstream educational settings are widely considered to offer children with autistic spectrum disorder (ASD) equal opportunities and the best preparation for real life. But, by their very nature, mainstream settings demand almost constant integrated use of the very three skills or attributes, namely communication, socialization and imagination, in which individuals with ASD have impairments. The ongoing effort required of them just to 'fit in' is therefore huge. Add to this the natural demands of the academic learning process, and it can be seen that the pressure on a pupil who is trying to fully integrate into the mainstream is immense.

Having observed many ASD students in a variety of mainstream educational settings, I have become aware that successful inclusion can only be achieved when we take into account their unique and alternative ways of thinking and viewing the world. To do this we need to adapt the often rigid methods employed in the mainstream environment, and be more flexible in our approaches. For regular teachers or support assistants, this can be quite a challenge, as close and intense working often hinders our ability to see the environment through the eyes of those with ASD. Because they may be hypersensitive to aspects of their environment, they may become overwhelmed or distracted, either simply switching off from the immediate surroundings and tasks or engaging in what may be perceived as 'inappropriate' behaviours. In these instances, however, such 'inappropriate' behaviours are far more likely to be self-comforting ones. Alternatively, such behaviours may be the only way a pupil can communicate his or her real needs and wants.

However, there may be, depending on the true nature of the child, some displays of behaviour that are just what they appear to be – inappropriate. Learning to distinguish the meaning of different behaviours leads to a better understanding of the pupil and his or her individual needs. Strategies and techniques are included throughout the book to support teachers in this differentiation.

Many mainstream schools have already begun to work in the alternative or adapted ways required to fully include those pupils with ASD. All schools can do this, both cost- and time-effectively, by consistently applying achievable, specialist interventions. This requires that all involved staff and parents work as closely together as possible.

Support from home, therefore, is essential. Parents and carers of pupils with ASD play an important role in reinforcing strategies that are being taught at school. Experience indicates that parents and carers are keen to become involved, and appreciate being kept informed of any strategies implemented by the school, no matter how seemingly insignificant. The fact that individuals typically do not transfer learnt skills in new settings and situations emphasizes the need for involvement by parents. Methods of achieving this level of co-operation are examined throughout the book, and particularly in Chapter 12.

Whilst most pupils placed in mainstream settings initially require a good deal of extra support, many, having been sympathetically guided to settle into their new school surroundings and routines, do become more independent. The strategies and information in the following chapters aim to support pupils in their ultimate achievement of this independence.

Note that many examples given throughout the book are 'worst case' scenarios. It is important to remember that individuals with ASD are affected to varying degrees, and no two individuals are affected in exactly the same way. For inclusion in the mainstream to be easy and effective, staff should only focus at any one time on one or two areas of difficulty that require immediate attention. Some pupils have difficulties that will require attention and special intervention for a longer time, or even in an ongoing capacity, whereas for others the process will be much quicker and easier. In all cases, the interventions must aim for realistic outcomes in an achievable time-frame. These are examined in detail in Chapter 12.

Many of the strategies described throughout the book initially require full support by staff, but are designed to enable gradual and discreet withdrawal of support, ultimately resulting in greater or complete independence and inclusion of the pupil with ASD. Many of the included strategies can be adapted and used with other pupils with similar behavioural or learning difficulties, which thus means that individuals with ASD are not necessarily singled out.

With an official diagnosis of ASD may come a statement of special educational needs (SEN). This can be viewed as a positive step towards ensuring adequate funding for in-school support; realistically, this is commonly not the case, with many schools either juggling other funding, or self-funding further support as deemed necessary. For this reason, all included strategies necessarily take into account the staff resources available.

For ease of reference, strategies within relevant chapters have been divided into two sections – pre- and primary school, and secondary school applications.

Finally, it is frequently surprising how much can be discovered about a pupil's real needs and wants with a little applied specialist effort. It is immensely rewarding when this effort not only results in a much happier pupil, but also in much happier staff, parents and peers.

History of autism

In Boston, USA, child psychiatrist Leo Kanner studied a group of 11 children (eight boys and three girls) whose behaviour he described as being 'markedly and uniquely' different to the majority. Although these children appeared physically normal, they each displayed an extreme aloneness or 'profound autistic withdrawal'. Kanner's paper, published in 1943 and entitled 'Autistic Disturbances of Affective Contact' refers to an 'infantile autism'. Nowadays, those individuals affected in a similar way are often referred to as 'typically' or 'classically' autistic. Striking features of this typical or classic autism include:

- A common inability to develop relationships – even with parents and siblings.

- Limited interactive skills, ranging from poor eye contact to an inability to converse, socialize or share.

- A preference for repetitive, stereotyped play, such as building towers of bricks, or laying out long lines of favourite objects – toy cars, books and so on – with no real idea of how the particular toy or object could be more appropriately used.

- A preference for and fascination with objects that can be easily handled with repeated fine motor movements, particularly those that can be made to spin, again with no idea of how to more appropriately use or play with the object or toy in question.

- An obsessive desire for the preservation of sameness, including routines.

- Extreme distress if routines are unexpectedly changed. This includes those rituals that are self-imposed to provide comfort but that may be socially inappropriate.

- An over-sensitivity to environmental stimuli; the response to stimulation overload may be to rock or cover the ears.

- Good rote memory skills, often relating to unusual subjects, such as shoe sizes, supermarkets, car registration numbers and so on.

- A marked delay or obvious failure in language acquisition.

- Unusual use of language in a non-communicative way.

In 1944 Hans Asperger, a pediatrician who lived and worked in Vienna, published a paper entitled 'Autistic Psychopathy in Childhood'. In it he describes a group of boys who had average or above average IQs, but who found it 'difficult to fit in socially'. Such children would be described by parents and teachers today as being 'academically bright but socially a little bit odd', or 'highly intelligent but a bit eccentric' or even 'cheeky, almost rude'.

In the playground, they often display a preference for solitary play, rather than joining in games with other children. The majority will become anxious or upset if there are unexpected changes in their day, such as lesson, room or teacher changes.

One of the striking features of Asperger's study group was that of pupils having the ability to speak fluently but with a common lack of understanding and ability regarding the importance and use of social conversation. This group commonly displayed speech that, although having good grammar content, articulation and wide vocabulary, was pedantic and stereotyped in delivery. Modern descriptions relating to this aspect of difficulty include one-sided conversations, monologue-type delivery and the inappropriate or unusual use of complicated or adult words. Some pupils are described as sounding very formal or stilted when speaking.

Another striking feature of this study group was that of all the boys frequently making attempts at socializing and approaching others but on doing so, typically making mistakes – modern descriptions also include 'not learning from their mistakes'. As well as lacking social skills, most of this group were noted to be poorly co-ordinated. Today, pupils are frequently described as appearing 'clumsy', and often have little understanding of 'personal space' issues.

Individuals within Asperger's study group were aware of being different, and some became depressed. Today, such pupils who are aware of these differences are often noted to have low self-esteem, may become tearful, depressed, and at times, suicidal.

Those 'classically autistic' individuals in Kanner's study group, and those individuals in Asperger's group shared some characteristics, most notably a tendency to have obsessive or unusual interests, and a preference for routine.

In 1979 Wing and Gould published findings of their study, carried out in Camberwell, which confirmed that, although autistic children showed a wide range of difficulties, there were three areas of impairment that could be commonly identified – in language and communication, social skills, and flexibility of thought or imagination. Consequently, Wing's 'Triad of Impairments' became the basis of diagnosis (see p.16).

Following Wing and Gould's study, a further theory, that people with autistic spectrum disorder (ASD) have impaired 'theory of mind' (which is the ability to understand others' mental states), was developed by Simon Baron-Cohen, Uta Frith and Alan Leslie.

Much work and research has been done and is still being carried out regarding all aspects of ASD. Although claims have ranged from 'miracle cures' to 'improvement can be achieved', the findings to date suggest that although autism can be managed with specialist intervention, it cannot be cured. If a person has autism, he or she will have autism for life. This will be in varying degrees for each individual.

The autistic spectrum

Although the individuals in Kanner's, Asperger's and Wing and Gould's study groups were all impaired to some degree in the areas of communication, imagination and socialization (now commonly referred to as the Triad of Impairments), there were noticeable differences, especially between Kanner's and Asperger's groups, many of which we have already examined. But because different approaches need to be applied to those with Asperger syndrome it is most important to recognize and identify those pupils affected by it.

Frequently-made social approaches, the ability to speak fluently and apparently knowledgably, together with average or above average IQ and proclaimed self-awareness, often results in a diagnosis of Asperger syndrome being delayed. In the context of a mainstream school environment this delay can result in huge difficulties for all involved. Furthermore, there are some pupils recognized who display many of the characteristics associated with ASD, but in a subtle way, and therefore have not been diagnosed (and may not be). They also require specialist intervention to help both them and their classmates if they are to achieve their best.

Common identifying characteristics of Asperger syndrome may include:

- average or above average IQ
- frequent displays of odd and inappropriate social behaviour
- literal interpretation of language
- fluent speech, often using complicated words
- extended monologues
- monotonous and formal or stilted speech
- appearance of egocentricity
- poor co-ordination
- an awareness of being different, particularly in older pupils
- being prone to low self-esteem and feelings of worthlessness
- a tendency to become depressed, or suicidal in extreme situations.

No two individuals are affected to exactly the same degree, and therefore each person is referred to as having an ASD; some, as already described, are further referred to as having Asperger syndrome.

Whilst a diagnosis of ASD can be made at any time, the most common age for the diagnosis of 'classic' autism is between 18 months and two-and-a-half years. For reasons already examined, the diagnosis of Asperger syndrome is generally later, usually between four and six years old, although it may be made well into adulthood. It is believed that some individuals with Asperger syndrome are never officially diagnosed, so subtly are they affected. It is also believed by some that we are all on the spectrum somewhere.

Recent research shows four times more males than females are affected by ASD, including Asperger syndrome. This replaces the long-held previous ratio of 10:1 (males to females) applicable to Asperger syndrome. The reasoning behind this is that girls with Asperger syndrome seem able to disguise their symptoms more effectively, and therefore may go undetected.

Nowadays, community paediatricians are commonly those who officially record a diagnosis of ASD. This is usually on the strength of their own observations of the individual, and in conjunction with information gathered from parents, schools and other professionals. These professionals may include speech and language therapists, educational psychologists and clinical psychologists.

Older, more able individuals – especially those with Asperger syndrome – frequently report relief at having finally received an 'official' diagnosis and recognition of their difficulties, no matter how subtle.

Early diagnosis of ASD to enable early interventions is generally viewed positively both by parents and schools.

The Triad of Impairments

To gain better understanding of how autism (including Asperger syndrome) as defined by Wing and Gould (1979) affects an individual we now examine the Triad of Impairments in more detail.

Communication

The skill of communication is an infinitely complex one. Besides the prosodic intricacies of verbal content (expression, volume and speed of speech) it includes those incalculable ones of eye contact, facial expression and gestures.

The inability to interpret, use and appropriately respond to communication is a difficulty regularly faced by all individuals with autism. Both for those who cannot speak, and those with Asperger syndrome who may be prone to making literal interpretations and/or giving long-winded monologues, effective and appropriate social communication is a constant challenge. For those in mainstream school settings such challenges inevitably occur countless times a day.

Whilst classically affected autistic individuals do not naturally make eye contact, those with Asperger syndrome who do so may be unable to make or interpret it correctly. Individuals may stare or look away at the most inappropriate of times, which, as well as creating obvious social difficulties, may also affect academic learning. No individuals with autism, therefore, are able to easily interpret this aspect of communication, in order to identify or appropriately respond to true verbal meaning.

For the majority of people, the natural reading and interpretation of gestures and facial expression leads to a more real understanding of what someone is actually saying. The inability to interpret these signals when combined with the spoken word may hinder an individual's perception of what is actually being said and, when applied to learning situations, exactly what is required. An individual's own inability to use appropriate gestures, verbal communication, eye contact and facial expression magnifies the difficulty. Some students, aware of being different but desperate to join in and blend with the rest, present a confident and knowledgeable façade, but actually have little or no real idea of what is required. Others, with no knowledge or confidence, prefer to withdraw.

Despite the difficulties encountered by all individuals with autism, improvements in communication can be achieved with specialist intervention.

Socialization

For the majority of people, the social aspect of life is often the part they enjoy (and are expected to enjoy) the most. Most school children love playtimes and making new friends. For those affected by more classic autism, who much prefer to withdraw from others to focus on objects, this is simply not the case. For those with Asperger syndrome, who desperately want to join in but on doing so typically make repeated mistakes, social situations of any kind may frequently result in frustration and distress. All individuals with autism are regularly challenged by their natural inability to decipher and react appropriately to different social situations. For pupils in a mainstream school setting, such social challenges occur many times each day.

Socialization impairments do not just affect an individual's ability to play and make friends. Within a school environment they also extend to small group or partner working, whole class address situations, contact or team sports, lesson change-over times, dining hall settings, quiet working times, teacher–pupil relationships and so on; in fact, any situation involving at least one other. In essence, life, especially school life, is mostly 'social'. It constantly involves learning how to mix and interact with others in a variety of settings and situations, on a variety of different levels. This social learning process does not just rely on direct verbal communication skills but also on picking up on and deciphering unwritten social cues and rules. For the majority, it is an ongoing, completely natural and exciting learning process. For all individuals with autism, particularly those with Asperger syndrome, it is a veritable minefield of one exhausting challenge after another.

Whilst, with specialist intervention, a pupil can be helped to acquire more effective socialization skills, the complex nature of the disorder requires that these skills may initially need to be taught in every new social situation or setting. As a pupil builds up a memory bank of 'real life tried and tested' successful social scenarios, he or she will become better able to respond appropriately in any given social situation.

Imagination

Imagination impairment greatly affects an individual's ability to pretend or become involved in otherwise imaginative or creative play with others, or to problem solve.

In addition, this impairment may also lead to individuals displaying a limited understanding of consequences, both positive and negative. Without actual experience of an event to provide a real life memory bank, the individual will be unable to conceive that something *might* happen, and therefore takes no heed of any verbal warnings or explanations, however detailed or lengthy.

Imagination impairment also frequently results in resistance to change of any kind. Within a school environment this 'rigidity of thought' typically prevents the transfer of any learnt skills or coping strategies. Each subject, just as for each new social setting, really is an entirely new and separate learning challenge for pupils. Moreover, these challenges, brought about by continual change, occur throughout the individual's entire school life from pre-school to the secondary years, and include the day-to-day variations in timetables, curriculum, physical locations, teachers, peers and expectations. The slightest change in usual routine may cause an individual to become upset for the rest of the school day. The majority of us can only imagine how exhausting it must be to have to struggle to constantly cope with so many frightening changes, in addition to contending with extra pressures of workloads and adolescence.

CHAPTER 1

Familiarization

There is no doubt an early diagnosis of ASD to enable early intervention is a positive thing. Early interventions ensure even very young children with ASD have a better chance of having their individual educational needs met. Nowadays this often includes supported placements in mainstream pre-school settings. In a bid to ensure all pupils, regardless of age, are fully prepared for their first full session at a new school or in a different year class, one of the most important strategies used is familiarization.

Because of their general resistance to change, all pupils with ASD derive benefit from certain aspects of this technique. Before we examine strategies for specific ages and settings, let us first examine more general ones, those useful for all pupils with ASD.

New intake

In the case of all pupils starting a new school the degree of distress or anxiety can be reduced by arranging an initial visit out of school hours. Provide parents with a photograph of the outside of the building, as this helps to prepare their child for the visit. Supplying one or two photographs of key members of staff further builds on this approach.

Even for purposes of this first visit it is advisable to use the exact entrance route into the classroom the child is expected to use when term begins. For some, this may include a visit to the cloakroom or locker room first.

During the initial visit, which should always include parent or carer, attending staff should be prepared for a child not to show great or appropriate interest. This issue should not be forced at this stage. Pupils commonly respond well if they have been allowed time and space to assess any newcomer from a safe distance. Depending on the individual, extended communication may or may not be appropriate during this first meeting.

Allow a younger child to wander and explore; this provides an opportunity to observe which toys or activities he or she is particularly interested in. These may later be used as incentives or rewards.

Depending on the individual's reaction to this first visit, further 'taster' sessions in and out of the classroom may be required. These may extend to include, at pre- and primary school stage, play and snack times, and at secondary stage, lunch-times. Introducing all pupils to midday supervisory staff should not be overlooked, as this is an important part of the familiarization process.

During the second visit, once the pupil has safely processed and 'memory banked' important staff, it may be reasonable to expect and encourage more in the way of social recognition and communication. For younger children, begin by encouraging them towards a toy or activity they previously showed an interest in. For older pupils, try easy conversation, an introduction to friendly peers, or inclusion in an enjoyable lesson.

Second visits are useful for familiarizing new intakes with other important physical facilities within the school, such as the dining hall, office, computer suites and so on.

Schools working inclusively with pupils with ASD recognize the need for sympathetic and individual introduction, and begin the familiarization process weeks in advance of when full-time attendance is due to begin. The availability of staff to support this, even for only thirty minutes a week, goes a long way to fully preparing an incoming pupil.

Change of schools

For some pupils, a change of schools can be extremely daunting. Both involved schools need to be prepared to work closely together to ensure a smooth transition. The same familiarization techniques should be used as for new intakes. For some pupils, this may initially mean missing the last lesson at the current school in order to visit the new school. As the familiarization process builds, other lessons, or indeed whole sessions, may need to be missed.

After the initial visit with parents, it is beneficial to arrange for the pupil's current support worker to help with subsequent visits. This is most useful for those times when pupils will be expected to join in with taster lessons. It also provides an ideal opportunity to begin a discreet handover of the pupil to the new support worker.

When pupils are coming from another school, an observational visit to their current school is a more effective way of establishing their individual needs than forging through written files. It also offers an excellent opportunity to observe successful teaching and support strategies. Using the same or adapted strategies later affords greater management consistency. Familiarization can again be aided by providing the current school with photographs of the new school to discuss with pupils.

During an observational visit to the current school setting it may be tempting to introduce oneself to the designated pupil, but it is important to remember the 'safe distance' process rule. However, some pupils (particularly those with Asperger syndrome) may independently approach a visitor. In this case, always be prepared for an odd social approach. Unless an individual has been specifically taught to say 'Hello', he or she may begin a conversation with something else entirely. One secondary pupil first approached me by asking my weight, another primary pupil by asking if I really loved Thomas the Tank Engine. The most appropriate way to deal with this is to say 'Oh! You mean "hello". Hello!' and then wait for a response. Depending on the response and classroom circumstance, further conversation may or may not follow.

In-school familiarization

More inclusively schools also acknowledge the need to familiarize those pupils within their school moving from one year class to another. A series of taster sessions will considerably reduce any anxiety about their new classroom and teacher. Depending on the individual, these taster sessions may be peer buddy or staff supported. In order to further encourage pupils, it is wise to initially choose those lessons or sessions a pupil may enjoy or are good at.

This type of familiarization should always include any new entrance and exit routes, different toilet and cloakroom facilities, dining hall seating arrangements and so on. From the outset, it is sensible to seat the incoming pupil where he or she will be seated the following term and, for some pupils, labelling a chair or desk with their name may help with their understanding of this. Visual timetables showing sessions in the new classroom also help to prepare pupils for this change in their usual routine.

Unless a teacher is already familiar with an incoming pupil, it is wise not to expect too much by way of social communication from him and her during the first visit. The new classroom surroundings and learning differences may be as much as an individual can easily cope with. For those with Asperger syndrome, who may be keen to socialize at any given opportunity, a good, fun way of setting behavioural boundaries from the start is to encourage them to produce a staff sheet of 'Classroom Rules' on the computer during their first visit.

'Behind the scenes' familiarization

This aspect of familiarization is particularly useful for those incoming pupils who staff have never met before. Gather information from parents by telephone if necessary about an individual's particular likes and dislikes and favourite lesson subjects, to provide an appropriate 'non-threatening' starting point for conversation during the first visit. It is also useful to find out a little about a pupil's special interests, so that relevant games, stickers, puzzles, worksheets, computer programmes and so on can then be available during initial meetings.

This information gathered from parents is just as important as that obtained from professionals involved with the child. Parent/school liaison is detailed in Chapter 12.

Peer/buddy familiarization

Having familiarized incoming pupils with their physical surroundings, the next stage is to introduce them to some of their peers and/or buddies. For younger pupils, it is useful to enlist the help of one or two understanding parents who are willing to allow their child to become involved by staying behind for 15 minutes or so after school. Alternatively, seek permission for supporting children to play quietly indoors during what would usually be outdoor playtime. For older primary pupils this type of familiarization may not be necessary, but for secondary pupils it is most advisable to introduce a buddy support system (further detailed in a later section of this chapter).

Before moving on to explore those familiarization techniques specifically for pupils in either pre- and primary school or secondary school settings, it is useful to examine *Real Life Memory Banking* (*RLMB*); this enables us to better understand why such sympathetic and individual pupil familiarization is so important.

Real Life Memory Banking (RLMB)

Because of their impairments, particularly in imagination, pupils lack the skills to predict the outcome of any new situation. When applied to a new school, teacher or classroom scenario this impairment typically prevents a pupil from foreseeing positive outcomes, no matter how much discussion there has been; only when the situation has been experienced can the pupil gain a true understanding of it.

Unfortunately, RLMB is not only confined to positive or enjoyable experiences. Some pupils build up entire banks of unpleasant memories. In extreme cases these can overwhelm a pupil (particularly one with Asperger syndrome) to the point of severe depression, withdrawal and, at worst, suicide.

It is of the utmost importance, therefore, that pupils are given as many opportunities as possible to experience favourable outcomes at school, in order to build up positive RLMB experience. In this way, they are able to see that outcomes can be successful, and are more likely consequently to engage willingly in new activities.

It is therefore important to ensure that any familiarization session ends on a highly positive note. Never extend the session beyond what you would consider to be a wholly positive experience for the child, remembering that RLMB may have begun the moment he or she walked through the door. Ensure that the environment and experience are as peaceful and non-threatening as possible; in this way, not only will the pupil gain confidence and be more co-operative, but he or she will have a successful 'tried and tested' real life memory bank experience to refer to in readiness for future sessions.

Familiarization techniques specific to pre- and primary school settings

- From the outset, encourage parents to let their child be physically independent of them. This may be something to discuss with parents before the first meeting. A well-intentioned parent 'clinging on' to a child (particularly during a first visit) may unwittingly set an obstructive pattern that is subsequently hard to break. The long-term aim of even this first visit is for a child to feel comfortable and confident at school *without* his or her parents by his or her side. Parental physical proximity is therefore something to be completely withdrawn if possible before a child attends regularly.

- Depending on school policy the ultimate aim is for the parent and child to say goodbye at the school gate, or door, in the playground. Subsequent taster sessions, therefore, should make provision for ensuring this is practised and fully supported by parents. In the event of pupil tears and tantrums during farewell time, the school can contact anxious parents by telephone later that morning. Experience proves that pupils settle far more quickly when Mum or Dad has disappeared from view.

- Depending on school policy, some parents may be welcome to stay with their child for all or part of the session, particularly at pre-school. This may make it more difficult for parents of children with ASD to accept that they *shouldn't*. More able pupils tell of a definite and comfortable divide between school and home. Feeling safer within known boundaries, pupils much prefer school to deal with school issues and parents to deal with those at home. To attempt to bridge this divide by encouraging parents to stay at school may therefore cause greater harm than good.

- Because of the obvious differences between morning and afternoon sessions, pupils should taste both before starting full time. This not only raises the child's awareness of what to expect, but also alerts teaching and support staff to the child's needs. A comparatively unstructured afternoon session may require more intensive staff support than a morning one. When support hours are at a minimum it is essential to arrange these to best suit an individual's real needs.

- First taster sessions should always avoid lesson change-over times. These are naturally noisy and chaotic, and another area through which pupils will need to be sympathetically, sometimes physically, guided.

- Lunch, snack and break-times are important, and should be included as part of the familiarization process. Indoor and

outdoor playtimes should also be included, as the routines and
expectations for these are very different.

- Some pupils may have several different support workers
throughout a week. Before full-time attendance, it is beneficial
to ensure pupils have been introduced to, and had the
opportunity to work with, each one. The sudden and
unexpected introduction of a new support worker (one who
has been away sick, or on holiday, for example) may easily
offset an unprepared pupil for the rest of the day.

- Familiarize pupils with a safe or quiet area within the
classroom that they can retreat to if necessary.

- Because some pupils may be expected to change uniform, or to
wear school uniform for the first time, the partial wearing of
this may be introduced during familiarization. For some pupils
this may be incredibly difficult – some may have a preference
for a particular colour or style of clothes; others may have
become so comfortable with their old school uniform that they
have no desire to change it whatsoever. If the wearing of
appropriate uniform is particularly difficult, consider
introducing just part of it to begin with. Also consider bending
the rules slightly regarding styles and shades of colours
initially; as a pupil's confidence in his or her new surroundings
increases, a more uniform dress code can be gradually
introduced. It is worth mentioning that some parents of
younger children with ASD physically struggle with their
child every morning just to get him or her dressed in *anything*
other than favourite pyjamas.

Familiarization techniques specific to secondary school settings

- Whenever possible, begin familiarizing secondary pupils in the
latter part of the term immediately proceeding the actual

intake term. The aim of secondary familiarization is to fully equip a pupil with everything he or she needs in order to settle easily into the secondary learning process from day one. Schools working inclusively with pupils with ASD acknowledge that buddy support systems are the easiest and most cost-effective way of helping with this. As pupil confidence and familiarization increases, these supports may be discreetly withdrawn.

- After an initial visit, subsequent taster visits should include change-over times, lunch-times and so on which are far less daunting to pupils when they are buddy-supported to begin with. Buddy supports may also be responsible for showing pupils how to use food and drink machines. These machines in themselves are often real incentives for pupils to attend; some schools work with parents to provide small financial incentives to use in these machines for good behaviour or a good week's work.

- Some pupils (particularly those with Asperger syndrome) may be reluctant to allow close proximity buddy support for fear of appearing too different. If this is the case, buddy supports can maintain a discreet distance in the corridor during change-over times. Should a difficult situation occur, buddies are then able to step in to help.

- Secondary pupils need a quiet or safe area or room to retreat to. This should always be included in the familiarization process, including some enjoyable time spent in it, perhaps with one or two others.

- Some secondary schools have a designated SEN staff room or office. This should also be shown during familiarization, together with any 'Help' notice boards that pupils need to be aware of, or expected to use. (Techniques to equip a pupil to use 'Help board' systems are detailed later, in Chapter 7.)

- Secondary schools working inclusively with pupils with ASD acknowledge the need to renew the buddy support systems at the beginning of each new term and, more importantly, each new school year. However, depending on the individual, this may only be necessary for a few days. Pupils with Asperger syndrome in particular are often prone to bullying by others. Experience proves that, despite best school efforts, many new pupils are bullied or teased within their first week at secondary school. If left unattended, this soon becomes the basis of a very negative unhappy experience of secondary school life. Aim to prevent RLMB experiences becoming overwhelmingly negative by providing adequate physical support initially, and reminding pupils of coping strategies they can use should difficulties occur.

- Flexible scheduling of support at the beginning and end of weeks and terms may be necessary initially to help pupils achieve greater independence. However, this re-scheduling of support may not necessarily only be confined to these times. Individuals with Asperger syndrome frequently report uncontrollable waves or tides of emotions sweeping over them. 'Keep a simple mood diary to pinpoint individual lows' and provide 'concentrated learning support assistant time during the lows' to help individuals to cope at these times (Attwood 2003). Whilst there can be no doubt moving to a new school or class may accentuate the lows, the adoption of suitable supporting techniques enables pupils to cope more easily.

- Some pupils may have to deal with new travelling arrangements. Discuss these with parents and pupils, and if necessary arrange practice bus or taxi rides in to school, supported by a staff member.

- For some pupils it may be useful initially for buddy supports to meet them at the school gates or an otherwise easily identifiable, designated outside area. As pupil confidence and orientation increases, this can be discreetly changed to appropriate internal school areas.

- At a time when peer pressure to conform peaks, those pupils who are aware of their differences may be prone to general low self-esteem, tearful outbursts and temper tantrums. These in themselves may attract unkind comments from others. Initially discuss highs and lows at the end of any taster session, as this will not only serve to erase distressing memories for the pupil, but also provide staff with a better understanding of what type of support will be required.

CHAPTER 2

Transitions in and around schools

Many pupils share a common lack of understanding regarding the importance of appropriate physical transitions within schools, often running, pushing through or displaying other inappropriate movements. This is especially noticeable during change-over times when individuals may become confused and/or frightened, but also likely at other times too. In extreme cases pupils may resort to obvious flapping, rocking or other self-comforting withdrawal behaviours, even at secondary stage. Besides attracting unwanted attention from unsympathetic others, this level of withdrawal makes it difficult for staff to refocus and settle an affected pupil to learning tasks.

Pupils are naturally unable to easily transfer and apply 'good walking' skills learned in other situations, such as at home, on family outings and shopping trips, or even those from previous schools. They may also have difficulty picking up on and imitating the acceptable ways that the majority moves. Schools working inclusively with pupils with ASD acknowledge the need for transition techniques and support strategies to be taught. In some cases, staff may need to initially physically guide or model these.

For those pupils preferring to withdraw, physical contact may not be appropriate. Pointing out others' good walking skills or the use of videos are useful techniques. Even very young individuals appear willing to watch and are able to learn appropriate social behaviours from TV and video prompts. This type of prompting is a completely non-threatening way of helping individuals to acquire acceptable skills. Some schools extend this type of media learning to videoing those pupils in need of specific behavioural support to encourage them to offer their own more socially acceptable alternatives. Appropriate suggestions are subsequently role-played to further enhance learning.

For those pupils who are easily distracted, visual prompts (such as a simple card with the name and photo of the teacher, the classroom number, and so on) may be required to remind them exactly where and to whom they should be going next. At secondary stage, it may be necessary for pupils to be allowed to move either just before or after the rest in order to maximize their confidence and achieve independent transition. Techniques to discreetly accommodate this provision of quiet corridor space are examined later in this chapter.

For all pupils, any change of location around the school is likely to first require a good deal of staff or buddy support in order to achieve the most acceptable and safe transition. As a pupil's confidence and understanding of expectations increases, support is discreetly withdrawn.

> The teaching of *any* new technique (transitional or otherwise) requires that the teacher has the full attention of the pupil. In the case of younger children especially, this may not be exactly when the teacher requires it. They must always be prepared, therefore, to use any opportunity when the pupil is paying full attention to respond to the most urgent behavioural or learning support needs. It is generally recommended that behavioural issues be approached before those of learning.

Having examined common transition difficulties, we will now explore those techniques suitable for specific ages and school settings.

Transitions within pre- and primary school settings

- Young children may need to be taught a good walking technique. For those willing to accept physical contact (if this isn't obvious, check with parents first – even some more classically autistic individuals will accept hand contact) this is most easily done by taking a pupil's hand to guide walking at an appropriate pace. The next stage of this technique is to withdraw the hand-held contact to place a guiding hand on the pupil's shoulder. Depending on the pupil's response, the physical support can then either be completely withdrawn or reverted to stage one (hand-holding). For those more reluctant to accept physical contact, it may be more appropriate to use a preferred toy or other object as a 'bridging device' to lead the child. The benefit with this technique is that staff can then offer playtime with the object as a reward afterwards.

- From the outset, staff must be firm and very clear about their expectations of good walking. If a pupil (especially one of primary age) *does* break into a run it is perfectly acceptable for staff to guide the pupil back to the beginning of the route. With pre-school pupils, who may have little or no previous experience of in-school walking, it may be advisable not to expect more than a few 'good' walked steps initially.

- As mentioned earlier, it may be more appropriate to teach some pupils good walking techniques by using videos or pointing out other pupils. Providing video or real life examples is useful initially even for those who accept physical contact.

- Verbally praise a pupil as he or she is displaying good walking to encourage continuation with it, and use stickers and other small rewards immediately afterwards. In the early stages, this may not necessarily be when staff are expecting to see, or trying to teach, a good walking technique. It therefore pays staff to be extra vigilant, and to praise *any* good behaviour they are focusing on teaching at the time in order to encourage future displays of it.

- Initially always ensure that a pupil has a *reason* to walk properly – for example, to a preferred toy or activity – as a further incentive.

- Because of difficulties in transferring learnt skills, some pupils may require good walking techniques to be taught in different locations within the school (dining hall, corridors, classroom, cloakroom etc.). It is unreasonable to expect a pupil who has only been taught to do this in the classroom to walk properly in the dining or assembly halls, for example, unless the technique has been specifically taught in these locations. As a pupil becomes increasingly aware of what is meant by 'good walking', staff are able to use this phrase to encourage it throughout.

- When moving from one room to another, some pupils (especially those who are easily distracted or tend to distract others) may benefit from a small hand-held card, not only to remind them where they should be going next, but also to physically occupy their busy hands. Write on it the name of the staff member or room they are moving towards. Instruct the pupil to hand the card to the receiving staff member on arrival in the new room. This then provides an opportunity to:

  o praise the pupil for his or her successful arrival, either verbally or with a sticker

  o give the pupil further instructions (e.g. to sit down, collect books etc.).

This technique also helps to avoid unstructured pupil 'free' time (no matter how brief) in which to resort to inappropriate behaviours. As with all new techniques, this particular one may initially require full support to be discreetly withdrawn later.

- In order to enable individuals to enter, leave or move within any particular room most quickly (for toileting, collection of necessary working materials etc.), point out the most uncluttered and less distracting route. For some this may require deliberately avoiding computer or sand/water play areas, for example. For others this may extend to avoiding certain other children. Praise a pupil for quick and successful completion of this type of transition, to encourage further displays.

- Pupils may need to be taught how to move around when the whole class is assembled on the carpet. Some, particularly those with Asperger syndrome, have a tendency to trample over others with little or no idea of how upsetting or painful this can be, and an inability to read and interpret even the most pained of expressions and exclamations. From the outset, provide a pupil with a designated area for carpet address, that is easily reached by an acceptable route.

Transitions within secondary school settings

- For some individuals, it may be more appropriate that transitions in secondary settings are supported by buddies rather than staff; in this way, the pupil does not appear to be so obviously different from others.

- Some pupils (particularly those with Asperger syndrome) may need to be taught how to enter and leave a room quietly. This is most applicable to those who have a tendency to imitate others' challenging behaviour in an attempt to fit in. Small, personalized weekly rewards and incentives (discussed and agreed with parents) help with this.

- Many pupils initially find change-over times extremely difficult to cope with. *I cannot stress enough how important it is that secondary schools recognize these times as potentially the most destructive for pupils (especially junior ones) with ASD.* The social pressures during these noisy and chaotic times, and the need to cope with room or building changes, can be overwhelming, even frightening. Individuals may be bullied or teased. Some may misinterpret accidental knocking into them as intentional bullying. Those with little idea of personal space issues may accidentally knock into other passing students but be accused of deliberately doing so. Unable to appropriately defend themselves – either verbally or physically – individuals may arrive at the next lesson completely distraught. Naturally reluctant or unable to explain, or clearly put into perspective their uncomfortable experience, some may withdraw into self-comforting behaviours for an entire lesson. Those who quietly RLMB one unpleasant change-over experience after another may well become depressed. At worst, because of change-over difficulties, pupils may refuse to attend school.

Secondary schools working inclusively with pupils with ASD acknowledge the importance of making adequate provision to ensure pupil safety and well-being during these times. *All* secondary schools can do this by considering the following:

1. Initially provide adequate buddy or staff support (as detailed in Chapter 1).

2. Encourage pupils to walk with sympathetic, well-behaved others from one lesson to the next (many classes split into separate level groups for certain subjects – therefore a number of different walking partners may be required).

3. Staff should never rely solely on a pupil's 'best' friend to always be there to help with transition, or indeed with any other needy situation. In the case of the best friend being absent from school, a pupil can quickly get into all sorts of difficulties. I know of a situation where total pupil dependence on only one other resulted in absolute refusal to attend until the ailing friend also returned to school. In this

case, upon the eventual return of both pupils two weeks later, it was necessary to start re-integration of the pupil for preferred lessons only, and to re-teach *all* earlier transition support strategies.

4. Staff should be aware that a pupil's own preferred choice of support might not always be the most appropriate support for school transitions. This is commonly evident in those with Asperger syndrome who often gravitate towards other equally lively or challenging pupils. One way to help with this whilst still respecting an individual's own preference is to provide discreet buddy or staff support from a distance. If a preferred walking partnership becomes obviously unsuitable, staff must realistically consider encouraging and introducing more appropriate others.

5. Allow a pupil to move before or after the majority during change-over times, to most effectively reduce anxiety and distress. This can be done most easily and discreetly by having a brief conversation with the pupil for a few minutes, or by engaging him or her in a small but important (and perhaps rewarded) task, such as wiping the board or stacking chairs. Depending on school preference, it may be more appropriate to allow the pupil to leave the room a few minutes early. Whilst some individuals may be confident of doing this alone, others may initially require peer or staff support. However this technique is applied, it generally assures much quieter corridors for a pupil to move through. It also provides a more private opportunity for those pupils who have a real need to indulge in self-comforting or anxiety-relieving 'in between lesson' behaviours to do so. (Information regarding other acceptable provision of pupil-preferred self-comforting behaviour time is detailed in Chapters 5, 7 and 9.)

6. Another common area of transition difficulty in secondary settings involves those pupils travelling to and from school by

bus. From the outset, ensure a pupil is seated as near to the driver as possible, to reduce and avoid distressing scenarios. Wherever possible, supply a 'bus buddy' initially. It is reasonable to quietly inform the bus driver of any potentially vulnerable pupils. Depending on the individual, it may be appropriate to encourage a pupil to read or engage in another suitable and enjoyable activity during travelling time. This is most useful for those who may otherwise use this time to engage in self-comforting activities, such as hand flapping. Whilst *some* travelling companions may be wholly sympathetic and understanding of these types of behaviours, there will be others who are not. Bus travelling techniques can be introduced during familiarization.

CHAPTER 3

Physical positioning

Pupils with ASD typically display poor concentration skills (unless focused on their special interests or obsessive behaviours), especially in large group situations, from which many would prefer to withdraw. Some with Asperger syndrome, however, aware of being different, feel an equal pressure to conform within the group. Others, who are liable to make literal interpretations and who have little understanding of verbal inferences, find group address situations particularly confusing. And for those who find comfort in their special interests or obsessive rituals, the distraction imposed by the group situation may be naturally upsetting.

Their inability to process large amounts of verbal information at any one time results in many pupils switching off or resorting to self-comforting behaviours during a verbal address. Frequently this results in their failing to fully understand the message and what is expected of them.

Because pupils are so easily distracted it is important to ensure that *all* distractions (especially during group address situations) are minimal. Schools working inclusively with pupils with ASD acknowledge this is most easily achieved by encouraging correct physical positioning. Before examining strategies for specific ages and settings, we first examine more general ones.

Classroom

It is generally recommended that pupils be seated towards the front of the class, within easy sight of the teacher and the chalk/wipe board. Some may be more appropriately seated by themselves, or with a well-behaved, quiet working partner. This is ideally something to be discussed and agreed during the familiarization process. Early preparation avoids those awkward situations whereby pupils may choose to sit at the back of class, as near to the computer or window as possible, or together with other lively, challenging pupils. Even older pupils benefit from sympathetic assistance and guidance concerning this. To attain as much consistency as possible in secondary settings where pupils use different rooms for different subjects, all staff should be made aware of suitable physical positioning, and encourage this initially. It is unreasonable to expect a pupil to naturally select appropriate seating from one room to another.

Younger pupils may benefit from having their chair or desk labelled with their name to assist in their understanding of physical positioning. Older ones can be encouraged to make a simple seating plan on the computer. Some individuals may require and benefit from a separate workstation area within a classroom environment. These are detailed in Chapter 5.

Some schools, especially those with a high percentage of SEN pupils but comparatively low resources in terms of support staff, have adopted 'big table' classroom layouts, often encouraging as many as eight or ten pupils with similar learning needs to sit together. Whilst these SEN tables are usually supported by staff, experience indicates they do not provide the best possible learning environment for those with ASD. Individuals (especially those forced to share their funded support workers with needy others) are typically seated with those children displaying challenging or disruptive behaviour. If the school is unable or refuses to provide optimum seating arrangements (that is, solitary or with one other – and there will inevitably be others within the class who would also benefit from this type of smaller seating arrangement), it may be far more appropriate to consider placing the pupil with ASD in a higher academic or better behaved group. In this way, individuals can still be given appropriate work to do, but in a more sympathetic working environment. Methods of encouraging pupils to work more independently in order for this technique to succeed are detailed in Chapter 5.

Assembly

Assembly situations are typically difficult for pupils to cope with. Many do not understand the importance or relevance of these, and some would much prefer to withdraw completely. Their common inability to pick up on important social cues may result in pupils behaving inappropriately. Schools working inclusively with pupils with ASD understand the real difficulties these pupils have during such times and, together with parents, often agree on a more manageable rate of participation such as two or three times a week. Rewards and incentives, such as time spent on the computer or in other preferred activities, can be used to encourage good behaviour in assemblies.

For some pupils, it may be reasonable initially to expect only a few minutes of good behaviour during assembly. This can be extended as a pupil becomes more confident. The type of assembly should also be taken into account. Some pupils will happily participate when the assembly is led by someone known to them, but have much more difficulty when it is led by a visitor. Others may be encouraged by subject matter or the songs.

It is advisable to seat all pupils with ASD on or towards the end of a row, preferably within easy reach and view of a member of staff. Should pupil concentration wander, the staff member is then quickly able to discreetly refocus or withdraw a pupil. Older primary and secondary pupils may benefit from buddy supports.

Some pupils benefit from using personal lyric sheets rather than being expected to follow the words on an overhead projector. Staff can encourage use of these sheets by supporting a pupil to photocopy and laminate them. The use of these sheets has the added bonus of occupying otherwise busy hands more appropriately, and may help those pupils who find it difficult to concentrate during assembly.

It is important to note that even a usually well-behaved pupil with ASD may have difficulty in coping with different situations within the assembly hall (e.g. visiting theatre company productions). Whilst early preparation goes a long way towards helping with this, it is unreasonable to expect a pupil to enjoy such situations or to participate as fully as one might hope. Full staff or buddy support, or alternative activities, should always be available for these times.

It is encouraging to note that however difficult assembly situations may initially be for some pupils, they are generally repetitive, almost ritualistic, in nature. Pupils soon become familiar with certain assembly routines and programmes. This in itself quickly lends itself to encouraging greater pupil confidence and co-operation.

Dining hall

School lunch-times are naturally noisy and chaotic. Some pupils find the crowds and sheer volume of noise unbearable at times. Others may take a dislike to certain smells. Unable to easily transfer learnt eating skills from home, some pupils (even older ones) may resort to eating with their hands or otherwise messily – for some this may even include taking preferred foods from, or spitting unwanted foods onto, others' plates. An inability to pick up on other unwritten social rules may prevent pupils from understanding they have to wait in line to be served or for their entire table to finish one course before being called to go for the next.

Those with poor co-ordination skills may have difficulty in scraping plates, stacking glasses etc. Others, who have reduced appetites due to an obsession with certain foods, or colours of food, prefer not to eat at all. Individuals with previous uncomfortable experiences of dining hall lunch-times may become equally reluctant. Schools working inclusively with pupils with ASD acknowledge the need for all pupils with ASD to have some degree of dining hall support available. This is most generally provided by ensuring a pupil is seated within easy proximity of midday supervisory assistant (MSA) staff or a support buddy.

Some schools further acknowledge that the provision of screened areas within the dining hall is initially the best way of teaching a pupil relevant social skills and behaviours. By doing this in a small group, supported by staff, individuals are not singled out. Having acquired the necessary skills, pupils can then be reintegrated with the majority. Those older pupils who are having difficulty with the dining hall situation, or those taking packed lunch to school, may benefit by being temporarily allowed to eat in the SEN safe or quiet room.

Having applied common physical positioning strategies, we can now examine those suitable for specific ages and settings.

Pre- and primary school settings

Carpet times

In order to most effectively reduce distractions while the teacher is using the board or big book, it is best to seat a child at the front of the group. Those with full support should be seated towards the side of the group to enable easy intervention by the support worker if necessary. In order that they derive most benefit from what the teacher is saying, it is generally recommended that pupils are actively encouraged from the outset to be as independent of their support workers as possible during carpet times. For younger children, or those showing preference towards a certain member of staff, this may initially prove very difficult. In these cases, support workers should either sit *beside* them on the floor, or on a chair at the edge of the group. Physical proximity can be gradually reduced as a pupil's confidence increases. Pupils should not be allowed to sit on the lap of the support staff, as this will inevitably create difficulties in encouraging physical independence later on.

Personal space

For some pupils, particularly those with Asperger syndrome, personal space issues may be a particular area of difficulty during carpet and assembly sitting times. Individuals have a tendency to fiddle with others' hair, clothes etc. To raise their awareness of personal space, some pupils may benefit from initially sitting inside a PE hoop covered in gold foil. This provides them with a very real and visual boundary. (It is commonly agreed that pupils with ASD often respond much better to the visual rather than verbal rule.) As pupil behaviour improves, the use of the hoop can be discreetly withdrawn. If the school *does* adopt this technique, it must also provide a suitable hanging place for the hoop when it is not in use.

Good sitting

Wherever physically positioned, younger pupils may need to be taught a good sitting technique. For times when they are seated on the floor, this is most easily achieved by instructing pupils to keep:

- bottoms on the floor
- legs crossed, or out straight – some have difficulty in crossing their legs
- hands in their laps.

For times when they are sitting in chairs, this should be adapted to:

- bottoms on their chairs
- feet on the floor
- arms folded.

Initially praise pupils at each successfully completed stage, which will further encourage them to continue gradually; then as pupils' understanding and awareness of expectations increase, praise and physical interventions by staff can be reduced until all that is needed is to ask pupils to show 'good sitting'. Good sitting techniques can be taught in a whole group format.

> It is important to remember that pupils may have difficulty transferring techniques and skills that they have learnt in one setting to another. It may be necessary therefore, especially for younger pupils, to repeat the teaching of various techniques – including 'good sitting' – in a whole variety of settings.

Physical withdrawal

Schools working inclusively with pupils with ASD acknowledge the need for the behaviour of pupils with ASD to be managed in much the same way as that of all other pupils. When applied to carpet times or whole class address situations, this sometimes requires the physical withdrawal of the pupil for all or part of the session. To achieve this most easily, the teacher and support workers should agree on a 'warning' strategy for older or more able pupils. This may be, for example, two verbal warnings by the teacher, followed by the withdrawal of the pupil from the group, to either sit beside the support worker, or completely apart from the rest of the group. Make *any* withdrawal time as uninteresting as possible (i.e. no verbal, eye or physical contact) to avoid pupils cunningly manipulating it in the future. To provide a consistent approach, and also to avoid pupils' confusion about behavioural expectations and consequences, it is important that withdrawal strategies (including where the pupil will be withdrawn to, and what sort of behaviour will be expected, e.g. good sitting) are known to be agreed upon by the teacher and support staff. It is further recommended that withdrawal duration time also be pre-agreed. For many, even one minute quickly helps improve pupil behaviour, especially if it is necessary to regularly repeat it initially.

Line up

Many schools have difficulties with pupils during line up times. Those preferring to withdraw tend not to want to join in, whilst those prone to egocentricity often insist on being at the front. For individuals prone to making literal interpretations, being told to 'Go to the back of' or 'Join' the line may cause further confusion. One of the easiest and most enjoyable ways to encourage good lining up behaviours and positioning initially is to call line up differently. This may include calling it in alphabetical order, or perhaps 'those wearing blue socks', 'those having names beginning with the same letter that starts the word *cat*', 'those who love Thomas the Tank Engine' etc. For some pupils, it may also be necessary to use pointing or physical guidance to the correct position. Initially teaching a good standing technique (feet still and hands by sides) further encourages more acceptable behaviour.

Secondary school settings

Whilst all important physical positioning strategies relating to secondary pupils have been included at the beginning of this chapter, the very nature of secondary school routine dictates that staff remain aware of the following:

- Pupils may need to be reminded of the best physical positioning for them with each new room change.

- Those pupils with a tendency to gravitate towards other equally lively and challenging pupils may frequently need to be discreetly encouraged to sit beside more appropriately behaved ones, or by themselves.

- Those prone to making literal interpretations may not be aware of inferred meaning when questioned by staff regarding physical positioning. One pupil – sitting towards the back of the science group and obviously unable to see the experiment being demonstrated – when asked by the teacher 'Can you see?' replied, 'Yes! Of course I can see! I'm not blind am I?'

- Agreeing on physical positioning with pupils and teaching staff before any new term begins helps to avoid potentially distressing outcomes later.

- At the discretion of staff, some pupils, having learnt appropriate behaviour and concentration skills while positioned at the front or at the side of the class, may eventually be given more freedom regarding positioning.

CHAPTER 4

Verbal instructions

Autistic thought processes typically prevent easy computing and interpretation of large amounts of language at any one time. It is important, therefore, to keep instructions short. For those prone to making literal interpretations it may be necessary to adjust the usual wording slightly, and avoid inference and double entendre. For those with associated semantic pragmatic disorders, it is frequently beneficial to *vastly* reduce and adapt the language used.

Whereas it is often necessary to adapt *instructions* for most pupils, it is reasonable and sensible to use more normal communication at other times. There will inevitably be ample opportunity throughout the school day to practise this.

Before moving on to examine the various difficulties individuals face, note that for *all* individuals the three golden rules for verbal instruction are:

1. *Keep it simple.*

2. *Be specific.*

3. *Be direct.*

Personal address

Pupils may not be aware the word 'everybody' includes them. Personally addressing a pupil by name before *any* verbal instruction will help secure his or her attention initially. To encourage attention during whole class or group address times it is useful at first to include a supporting phrase: for example, 'Steven. The word *everybody* includes you.' This can also be used with others within the group and, once a pupil has learnt to respond, be withdrawn.

Having secured the pupil's attention initially it is often useful, especially in the early teaching stages, to go and verbally praise and/or give a simple 'thumbs up' sign as a visual reward and confirmation of appropriate pupil response. Praise can be discreetly withdrawn as a pupil's understanding increases.

Literal interpretations

Avoid the use of questions such as 'Can you…?', 'Shall we…?', or 'Do you want to…?' as this will invariably elicit an honest but often inappropriate yes/no reply. Use a more direct verbal approach such as 'Marie. [Please] sit down [now]', which gives a pupil a much better understanding of the exact requirements.

For some pupils, it may be necessary to adapt worksheet wordings, as well as adjusting verbal language. A pupil with Asperger syndrome, having been given a worksheet entitled 'My best friend' (implying a human one in school), studiously proceeded to write about a dog. When the teacher questioned him about this he replied, 'Dog is man's best friend.'

Alternatively, spend a few minutes going through worksheets or task expectations with a pupil which will increase the likelihood of the pupil completing the activity appropriately and independently.

Semantic pragmatic disorder

Some individuals may have associated semantic pragmatic disorder (SPD). In these cases it is most beneficial to reduce all instructional language to a bare minimum. Whilst deliberately avoiding the use of words such as please and thank you may at first seem improper or uncomfortable, for those with SPD even *one* excessive or irrelevant word may cause confusion. The following is an example of the way a typical request to sit down may be interpreted by someone with SPD:

Sally	*Me*
Would	*Wood*
You	*Not me, you*
Like	*Similar*
To	*Two*
Sit	*Sit*
Down?	*Feathers?*

In this particular case, the request would therefore be more appropriately worded as 'Sally. Sit.'

Three-step prompt

It may be necessary initially to use pointing gestures and/or physical guidance with some pupils, especially when verbal instructions are minimal. Because some individuals do not use or understand the importance of pointing, and because others may be reluctant to accept physical guidance, a three-step prompt technique, which allows pupils three separate and different opportunities to respond, is the easiest way to do this:

1. 'David. [Please] sit down.'

2. Repeat of verbal instruction, together with pointing to indicate where to sit.

3. Repeat of verbal instruction, together with physical guidance to indicate where and when to sit.

Remember to allow a few extra seconds of processing time for *all* ASD pupils before expecting *any* response. Also, whenever staff *do* find it necessary to repeat a verbal instruction, they must always ensure they use exactly the same wording each time. A change to even *one* word may be interpreted by some pupils as a completely different request altogether.

Staff intonation, facial expression and body gesture

Some pupils may be unable to interpret even the most urgently intoned of verbal instructions. Raising one's voice to some individuals may have the unwanted effect of encouraging those individuals to raise their own even louder. In extreme cases, pupils who hear their name 'shouted' often, or frequently followed by disciplining comments, may eventually refuse to respond to it at all. Their inability to read and interpret body language and facial expression may further prevent pupils responding appropriately.

Therefore, to encourage a pupil to co-operate most fully with *any* verbal instruction, always speak as calmly as possible – even in the most urgent, demanding or frustrating of situations; and do not rely on the pupil's ability to understand other forms of communication. Supporting programmes to assist in a pupil's understanding of these are generally accessed via School Support Teams (SSTs) or speech and language therapists.

Word audits

Some individuals – especially those with SPD, but also some with Asperger syndrome – may have a different or limited interpretation of verbal language. This impairment may prevent pupils responding appropriately, despite simple, repeated instruction. It is often beneficial to regularly 'word audit' pupils.

One example of the importance of this at secondary level involves a Year 7 pupil who, despite otherwise offering excellent written English assignments, never included capital letters at the beginning of a sentence, but often inserted them between sentences, after the full stop at the end of one sentence, and before the beginning of the next. Whilst this initially resulted in his teacher striking his mistakes with a red pen, it ultimately resulted in the pupil's refusal to attend school on the days of his English lessons. When auditing this particular difficulty with him, the teacher simply asked him, 'Where do capital letters go?' He replied, '*Before* a sentence.' The teacher pointed out that they actually went at the *beginning* of a sentence, and also encouraged him to write, under supervision, three sentences which contained correctly placed capital letters. This quickly assisted his understanding, and ultimately increased school attendance.

An example at the primary level of the importance of word auditing involves a pupil who, despite being taught and encouraged to supply appropriate wording of his own playground rules (including 'No thumping'), continued in his playful but painful thumping of others. On one occasion the pupil adamantly denied that he had thumped a female classmate, despite being seen by staff. When discussing this with him, I noted he used the word 'punch'. When asked to model the difference between a 'thump' and a 'punch', the pupil kept his thumb inside his clenched fist for the former, but outside for the latter. To him, there was a real difference between the two! Once his playground rules were adapted accordingly, there were no further instances.

Experience suggests that many pupils with ASD want to do well (and are capable of doing extremely well) at school, not only academically but also, in some cases, socially. Adapting and auditing instructional language – both verbal and written – goes a long way to assisting in this. Unfortunately, even the smallest of difficulties in language interpretation may have unwanted and confusing outcomes. It may be very useful, therefore, to regularly timetable into a pupil's weekly schedule some 'word audit' time – even for ten minutes daily or weekly – to address continued areas of difficulty.

Depending both on the individual and on the availability of staff, this can be scheduled during break/lunch-times, assembly or other such suitable times. Once these language interpretation difficulties have been identified and addressed, this time is discreetly withdrawn.

CHAPTER 5

Workstation areas

Having so far examined only a few of the most common areas of difficulty experienced by ASD pupils in mainstream settings, we begin to gain a better understanding of the amount and intensity of challenges these individuals face on a regular basis. Pressure on pupils to socially 'conform' and 'perform' is constant and immense.

One way of alleviating this when the pupil is trying to concentrate on written work is to provide a pupil with a workstation area within the classroom setting. Schools working inclusively with pupils with ASD recognize the need to provide *all* ASD pupils with some form of quiet working area to retreat to as required. This can be achieved in several affordable ways, examined later in this chapter. For those preferring to withdraw, it offers obvious privacy from others. For those much preferring to socialize, it notably reduces distractions. For *all* individuals, it enables greater focus and concentration on the working task.

Depending on the individual, quiet working may initially need to be staff supported, especially if a full workstation area is being provided. As pupils' understanding of how to use a workstation area increases, support can be discreetly withdrawn. Some pupils may only require a quiet working area for those subjects they have particular difficulty in.

From the outset, it is important to avoid using *any* quiet working area as a 'withdrawal/disciplining' or 'free time' space as well. This frequently confuses pupils as to its true intention, later promoting reluctance to work in it.

It is relevant to explain to others within the class that they must be wholly respectful of the fact that the area is a real working and learning need of a pupil with ASD. It is further relevant to explain that *whenever* a staff member is supporting a pupil in a designated quiet working area, he or she should not be interrupted.

> Despite the intentions of the staff to fully support a particular individual, other pupils in the class, even very young ones, quickly learn that they, too, can ask support staff for help, often at the most inopportune of times. Whilst many contractual agreements contain a covering clause for support workers to also provide 'other pupil support as necessary', it is unreasonable to expect this during designated, focused one-to-one time with the pupil with ASD. The easiest way to avoid interruption and confusion is to have prior agreement as to exactly when one-to-one and general class support times will be.

Whatever the type of workstation, the area immediately surrounding it should be as uncluttered as possible. For some, this may mean having nothing other than essential working materials to hand. For others, it may extend to a visual timetable, in- and out-trays etc. (detailed later in the chapter). In all cases, it should not be positioned near windows, computers or otherwise visible and easily accessible distractions, such as toy/activity boxes, etc.

When the workstation is not in use, staff and others must avoid it as a storage area for coats, handbags, books etc. (no matter how temporary), as this may cause a pupil to become distressed, confused and reluctant to use it. For those pupils requiring a full workstation area it is most beneficial to install it prior to and in readiness for the first day of the new term or year group.

Whenever providing any private/independent working area it is important to take into consideration the proximity of the electricity supply. Individuals may have an obsession with sockets and/or switching lights on and off. If it is impossible to position a quiet working area elsewhere within the room, then for safety reasons empty sockets should be child-proofed and switches taped. Alternatively, both the sockets and switches should be clearly labelled with a sign that indicates 'Do Not Touch'.

Recalling our aim of more inclusive mainstream schooling it is reasonable to expect and encourage *all* pupils using quiet working areas to also participate in small groups and whole class address situations. For some, this may only be for a few minutes initially. For other individuals, it will be for much longer periods. (Specific strategies to support the physical integration of reluctant pupils are examined in Chapters 7 and 8.)

Quiet working areas

Shared desk

Some pupils may benefit from simply having their own shared desk space taped or otherwise marked out. This is particularly useful for those pupils who generally work well once set to task but have a tendency either to fiddle with the belongings of others nearby, or become upset when others, even accidentally, do the same with theirs.

Private desk

Some individuals may benefit from having their own private desk. Depending on the individual this can either be positioned at the front of the class facing the teacher, or to the front and side of the room facing the wall. The provision and accessibility of seating for support staff should also be taken into consideration.

Screened areas

For some, it may be beneficial to partially screen a private desk area. This is useful when there is no other available, or suitable, space in the classroom. It also has the added benefit of being portable and accommodating of room change-overs and general classroom furniture moves. Different-sized partition screens are available from educational/office suppliers. Whilst specialist suppliers also offer prefabricated workstations, these are invariably more expensive and, depending on the amount of time individuals will be using them, may not warrant the expenditure. However, if the school has a high percentage of other pupils that may also benefit, or a pupil deemed to have a long-term need of a private workstation, this type of accommodation may be viable.

Techniques and equipment for use in workstation areas

Name labelling

Some pupils may benefit from having their quiet working area labelled with their name. To assist in a pupil's understanding of a particular area being his or her own workspace, staff can help the pupil to make a label, either by hand or on the computer. An example of appropriate wording might be 'Sean's quiet work desk'. For some, it may be necessary at first to explain and demonstrate exactly what 'quiet working' is.

In- and out-trays

For some pupils, it may be useful to provide in- and out-trays for their work, in a bid to avoid overwhelming them with too much visual information at any one time. Unless using a stacking system, where the in-tray goes on top, it is generally recommended that in-trays sit on the left of the desk, out-trays to the right. At the beginning of each day/session, staff can place worksheets and books in the in-tray in the order they will be needed. This has the obvious advantage of not only helping to keep a working area tidy, but also of providing pupils with a real visual sense of working achievement, especially as they see their out-tray becoming fuller and their in-tray emptier. A further advantage of this technique is that staff are able to discreetly substitute, withdraw or add any relevant worksheets where necessary. Pupils can be encouraged to make labels for the trays.

When first introducing this technique, especially to younger pupils, it is advisable to use only one or two worksheets at a time. For some, it may be useful and appropriate to offer a reward between completed worksheets. Others may need physical guidance to place completed worksheets in the out-tray. As pupils become more co-operative and familiar with the method, tasks and expectations can be increased accordingly. When first starting to teach this method, it will be necessary to remind pupils to stay in their seats and raise their hands once each worksheet has been completed, so that the staff member can guide them through the correct process. Whilst this initially requires vigilance and a prompt response by the staff, this extra help can be discreetly withdrawn as the pupil becomes more competent.

Visual timetables

Many pupils benefit from being supplied with a visual timetable in their quiet working area. For some individuals it may be more appropriate to supply separate ones for morning, mid-morning and afternoon. These can then be incorporated in the in- and out-tray method by pupils turning over or posting away the relevant timetable card to provide them with further visible confirmation of their systematically working through the school day. The importance and different types of visual timetables are examined more thoroughly in the next chapter.

Work materials

To begin with, provide pupils with their stationery requirements in small pots for use at their workstation rather than expecting them to retrieve what they need from larger shared trays or drawers within the classroom. For those preferring to withdraw from others, such an intrusion into their quiet working time may cause considerable distress. For those pupils much preferring to socialize or those who are easily distracted, such moving around the classroom may make it difficult for them to refocus on their task. For *all* individuals, it is best to avoid any distraction from the quiet working area and task, especially when applied to those subjects they would much prefer not to be doing. The small stationery pots should be stored out of sight and reach until required.

As pupils become more able, staff can discreetly begin to encourage individuals to collate their own work materials as appropriate.

In order to gain the maximum co-operation from pupils, and ensure that they have a good understanding of the proper use of materials, it is advisable to provide only the minimum amount of work materials and equipment, even in the secondary classroom setting. Large trays of counters and pencils, test tubes and thermometers, etc. invariably prove irresistibly tempting to pupils who are liable to misuse them.

Classroom withdrawal for quiet working

Some schools have a policy of regularly withdrawing pupils with ASD from the classroom for 'quiet working'. Whilst this can be *temporarily* useful for addressing particular areas of learning difficulty, and useful for the introduction of small and sympathetic group working, it often first occurs as a response to a pupil's inappropriate behaviour in the classroom. Unwittingly, this behaviour is rewarded by withdrawing the pupil from the class. The continued use of this strategy is frequently justified by schools as necessary to prevent others in the classroom being disturbed.

For those pupils *preferring* to withdraw, removal from the class may indeed have been their original intention. For those wanting to join in, but confused by lengthy verbal instructions, unkind comments from others and their own repeated mistakes, it is frequently easier and ultimately far more rewarding to manipulate comparatively 'safe', one-to-one withdrawal time by displaying 'inappropriate' classroom behaviours.

It is reasonably easy to distinguish between withdrawal time that is necessary, and that which is manipulated by the pupil, by noting how individuals respond during this time. Those who have *manipulated* it will subsequently use it to indulge in preferred self-comforting behaviours, which may include flapping, body rocking, crawling on the floor, or even determined (but irrelevant) conversation. Those who *need* it can inevitably be settled to work more easily. (Secondary schools working inclusively with pupils with ASD recognize pupils' real need for quiet working time by providing supervised, 'safe' working rooms for pupils to use, either during lesson times or at break-times.)

If the school *does* find it necessary to withdraw an individual from the classroom for quiet working, it is beneficial to regularly timetable it in and to support relevant areas of difficulty. At the discretion of staff, pupils may also be allowed (after completion of their work) to privately indulge in self-comforting behaviours prior to their return to the classroom.

Before any withdrawal from the classroom for quiet working, pupils should be made fully aware of *exactly* what the time is to be used for, the duration, and also of the need to return to the classroom later.

Before deciding to withdraw a pupil from the classroom for working, staff must also fully consider alternative working locations. Even a reasonably quiet library may be frequently visited by unsupervised groups of busy, chatting pupils. Likewise, a corridor area may continually stream with individuals moving from place to place. Whilst the use of a free head teacher's office may appear to offer an excellent quiet working environment, the possibility of interrupting telephone calls or irregular availability because of meetings, etc. must be considered.

In conclusion, unless others are in real physical danger, or there really *is* a more consistently quiet and suitable working area outside of the classroom environment, workstations within the classroom should be considered as the most inclusive and mainstream option.

CHAPTER 6

Visual timetables

Besides being useful for those pupils who require designated quiet working areas, visual timetables provide for *all* pupils with ASD an easily deciphered overview of the order and structure of the school day. For those preferring to withdraw from others, a visual timetable is the easiest way to discover what is happening. For those prone to distraction, it helps to refocus and remind them of appropriate tasks and expectations.

Whilst some pupils derive most benefit from being supplied with personalized timetables, at least to begin with, others may, at a later date, derive equal benefit from being encouraged to use a whole class one. Schools working inclusively with pupils with ASD recognize the need to provide *all* pupils with ASD with some form of visual timetable. For those pupils now progressed to using the whole class one, this may extend to encouraging him or her to be responsible for displaying/posting away relevant timetable cards. In instances of two or more pupils with ASD in the same class, this responsibility can be shared throughout the day or week, and, if appropriate, rewarded.

As well as providing pupils with a sense of structure, visual timetables are also excellent tools for staff, who are then able to forewarn and prepare pupils of any unexpected timetable changes. This is especially important at those times of the year when usual timetables are dropped in favour of sports day, the Christmas play and various end-of-term productions and practices. For pupils in particular year levels, these timetable changes also include national assessment, such as SATs and GCSEs. Staff can also use the relevant timetable cards as visual support for their verbal instructions when refocusing pupils who are wandering physically or mentally.

Visual timetables inevitably require staff time and effort to construct and teach, but invariably help pupils to become more independent. Laminate the timetable cards, as an affordable way to ensure their durability. Initially, pupils will need to be taught exactly what individual cards mean before they are able to respond most appropriately. For some pupils, there will need to be a very gradual introduction to the concept, beginning with only one or two cards a day or a week, before increasing to a more comprehensive whole session or whole day system.

Whenever using *any* visual timetable system – for one session only, or for an entire day – it is beneficial to include a special 'preferred' activity or time for the pupil to work towards; it will also be necessary to point out the inclusion of this special time to reluctant individuals. Examples of preferred time may be snack or lunch time for some; for others computer or reading time. If a particular session doesn't automatically include such a preference, it may be necessary to timetable one in at the end, if only for a few minutes. This may then be used as an incentive or reward for the pupil to complete other less enjoyable or difficult tasks first. As the pupil becomes more confident and co-operative, this preferred time is discreetly substituted with more appropriate, inclusive alternatives.

It is generally recommended that a visual timetable system should be continued once it has been established, even when a pupil appears not to need it any more. This is especially important at the beginning of each new term, year group or class. Many pupils regress to previous inappropriate behaviours after such a change, even though they may have become confident and co-operative in their former class. For some, this may happen after a prolonged period of absence, such as illness or holiday.

Management and use of timetables

- *Layout and constructional timetable.* Visual timetables should be
worked from left to right. Cards may be fixed with Blu-tack or
Velcro onto a laminated back sheet or pegged onto a string.
Depending on the needs of the individual, the cards may
depict the subject or the instruction with simple line drawings
with the corresponding word underneath; with words only;
with pictures cut out from magazines to illustrate which toys
or activities may be used; or with actual working materials, e.g.
crayons, paintbrushes, etc. This last method is especially useful
for younger pupils. Some schools include the use of
photographs, which are most useful for depicting *constant* daily
activities, people or working materials (such as home time,
one-to-one instruction, computer time, etc.), but should not be
relied on to support naturally *changing* times (outside play,
small group working, etc.), as even the re-positioning or
absence of a single photograph may cause an individual a
degree of confusion or distress.

- *Setting up and storage.* Staff will need to set up the visual
timetable system initially, on either a daily or
session-by-session basis. Later, depending on the ability of the
individual, it may be appropriate to involve the pupil by
guiding him or her to find the relevant cards. Reward
co-operation verbally or with a sticker to further boost and
encourage individuals. As a pupil becomes more familiar with
the order of events in each session (e.g. registration/
literacy/snack), he or she can assemble and place the cards
independently. Avoid providing pupils (and staff) with *too*
many cards to choose from. (I have known one nursery pupil
with literally a hundred to choose from. By the time
supporting staff had found the relevant carpet time card, carpet
time had finished.) However, it will be necessary (especially for
older primary pupils) to offer a variety of cards for each week.

To begin with, where pupils are selecting the cards independently, offer only one or two days' worth so that they have a greater opportunity to choose the right ones. As individuals become more capable, other cards are introduced. Because there will inevitably be cards that aren't required for particular sessions, it is sensible to provide a small storage box/tub for these. Pupils may be encouraged to help label this and, if appropriate, also informed of where it is kept.

- *Working through the timetable.* When a depicted task or lesson has been completed, a pupil is encouraged to either turn over the corresponding timetable card, or alternatively post it away in a box. Either way, this gives individuals a real visual sense of *fait accompli* and working through the day. When a posting box is used, it is stimulating for pupils if it is decorated with pictures of their special interests; where staff time permits, pupils may be encouraged to decorate and label it themselves.

- *Positioning of timetables and related equipment.* Timetables and posting boxes should be made easily accessible to pupils. Whilst some will be set in quiet working areas, others may be displayed elsewhere in the classroom. Unfortunately, notice board or free wall space is often at a premium, and some schools therefore tend to use cupboard ends or doors. Natural classroom business and the curiosity of other pupils often result in timetable cards being knocked off, misplaced or lost. To the pupil who relies on these timetable cards, this may cause a great deal of distress and confusion. It is therefore vital to ensure visual timetable materials are displayed in the most suitable *quiet* area.

- *Pocket-size timetables.* Older primary and secondary pupils (especially those with Asperger syndrome) may be most comfortable using a discreet pocket-size timetable. This type of reminder may also be used as a natural progression towards greater independence for those no longer apparently needing more obviously displayed ones. Whilst some school homework diaries include a timetable page, many pupils don't refer to them or have them easily accessible. Some pupils, especially those struggling with homework, much prefer to avoid looking in their homework diaries at all. In extreme cases, homework diaries (and, therefore, included timetables) mysteriously go missing. Consequently, some pupils also do – especially from those lessons or subjects with which they are having the most difficulty. The provision of a pocket-size timetable, together with staff or buddy intervention initially to encourage individuals to refer to the timetable, helps to avoid such possibilities. Suitably sized timetables can be produced on the photocopier, and later laminated. In this way, staff are still able to utilize original timetable cards but reduced in size. Depending on the needs of the individual and on the timetable schedule, these may be supplied on a daily or whole week basis.

- *Personalizing visual timetables.* We have already examined the possibility of including preferred interest time in visual timetables. This can be used as a reward or incentive for pupils to complete less enjoyable tasks and activities. As an extension of this idea, some pupils may benefit from having other 'less appealing' information visibly displayed. An example of this is outdoor playtime, as in the following situation. Throughout Year 7, a pupil was perfectly happy and willing to participate in outdoor playtime. At the beginning of Year 8, he was told by an interested but misguided classmate that, because he had sneezed during outdoor play, he might have hay fever. As a consequence, the pupil began refusing to go outside. This ultimately resulted in staff allowing him to spend every playtime indoors, in order to avoid the temper tantrums and displays of physical aggression he suddenly became prone to whenever it was suggested he play outdoors. This continued until Year 9, when specialist intervention was requested. The pupil was encouraged to produce on the computer a revised timetable to include five minutes of outdoor playtime in his daily schedule. It thereby became a very visual, and therefore real, rule, which quickly encouraged him to participate once more in outdoor playtime.

- *Updating timetables.* It is sensible to monitor timetables regularly, perhaps every term or half-term. Encourage pupils to revise them or produce new ones, especially if any permanent staff or room number changes have occurred.

CHAPTER 7

Other visual prompts

As we have seen already, pupils typically respond better to visual rather than verbal prompts and instructions (i.e. if they can see it or touch it, it must be real!). For those preferring to withdraw from others, visual prompts are the least threatening way to provide direction and structure. For those easily prone to distraction, visual prompts provide the staff and pupils involved with tangible reminders of both task and behavioural expectations. Because *all* individuals share communication difficulties, some form of visual prompt may need to be provided to support change of any kind.

Depending on the individual, the types of visual aids detailed in this chapter may need to be used initially in conjunction with adapted verbal instructions, visual timetables and/or three-step prompting techniques. Other pupils, however, may not require such fully supported visual direction.

It is important to remember that, because of the tendency of pupils with ASD to lack generalization skills, all visual prompting techniques may need to be taught or engineered in a whole variety of different subjects and settings.

Timers

Pupils typically have difficulty understanding the concept of time. Some may display this as a reluctance or stubborn refusal to move from one activity to another. This is especially apparent when attempting to move younger pupils from a preferred choice activity to a less appealing one. In other cases, the amount or quality of written work the pupils produce may be affected. (Further strategies to help with this are examined in Chapter 8.) Some pupils become obsessed with time, which staff must recognize *may* be due to a previous, unpleasant, RLMB experience where time was allocated verbally but not used appropriately.

Whilst it is important to verbally forewarn *all* pupils at least one minute before any impending change, others may require the support of visual prompts. As a pupil's understanding of time increases, these are discreetly withdrawn.

Suitable prompts, which should be portable, affordable and accessible, may include egg timers, stop-watches and/or other sand or even oil/water timers. For older, more capable, pupils it may be sufficient and more appropriate to point out the end of task time on the classroom clock or their own watch.

As well as having the time for written tasks visually prompted, some pupils may require that a range of other activities are prompted in this way. These include the toileting, changing, end of breaktime, withdrawal, disciplining and preferred behaviour 'free' time.

Stop and Tidy

Individuals often respond to being shown a 'Stop and Tidy' card. This is especially useful after activity times with younger pupils, although some older individuals may also require similar prompting after science experiments, art activities etc. For those regularly using visual timetables, a 'Stop and Tidy' card is inserted as required. As with *any* prompt card, staff may first need to teach its exact meaning. For younger or more reluctant pupils, it is reasonable to expect only the most fleeting of 'stops' and 'tidies' to begin with. Praise the tidying of even one brick or book, as this is the positive foundation on which to build greater pupil understanding and co-operation. As such moments of co-operation increase, the staff can raise their own expectations until the behaviour is commensurate with the majority.

Changing for PE

Pupils commonly experience difficulty with this. For those preferring to withdraw from others, the pressure of having to share a noisy, busy changing room can be immense. For those keen to socialize, the distraction from the actual clothes-changing task is equally huge. Pupils who are aware of being 'different' or who are poorly co-ordinated may be particularly reluctant and distressed. Some pupils, even older ones, may be unable to change themselves without some physical intervention by staff (see 'Backward chaining'). Others may be physically capable, but unaware of the correct and easiest changing order.

Provide pupils with two separate cards. The first one illustrates the sequence of changing from uniform to PE kit, the second one the reverse (PE kit back to uniform). Alternatively, provide a more detailed list of the order in which clothes should be changed (e.g. shoes off, sweatshirt off, etc.). If clothes-changing difficulties continue, staff may consider allowing pupils to change before or after the majority, or in a small sympathetic group situation.

Backward chaining

Whilst this is not a visual prompt *per se* it is relevant to include it as such, because of the difficulties some individuals may have with even specially adapted verbal instructions. Even some older pupils may need a degree of physical intervention to help with clothes changing, and to encourage the most appropriate and independent completion of this, a backward chaining technique is used. The amount of physical intervention required initially is wholly dependent on the degree of difficulty a particular pupil is experiencing. For all pupils, this will be different. For many, especially the younger ones, repeated physical interventions may be required at certain stages.

Full intervention at the first stage, for example, might involve removing a pupil's sweatshirt until it is almost over his head. The pupil is subsequently encouraged to complete the last stage of removal himself. With younger pupils even this action may require physical assistance. It is important to praise the pupil, verbally, or with a thumbs up gesture, for a job well done.

The next stage, once the pupil is able to complete stage one, is for the staff member to remove the pupil's sweatshirt without removing one (or both) of his arms from the sleeves. The staff member then encourages (and assists) if necessary the pupil to complete the task successfully before praising him.

The final stage is for the staff member to remove only the smallest part of the sweatshirt (e.g. beginning to lift the waistband), before encouraging the pupil to complete the removal of the sweatshirt independently. Once again, the pupil should be praised when the task is successfully completed.

It may be later necessary to repeat this entire process in reverse with some pupils. However, because many pupils with ASD respond well within known boundaries, and to set routines, and because some jump straight from stage one to stage three, this will not by any means be needed for all pupils; and if it is required, it may not take very long.

Before considering adoption of this technique, staff must also consider an individual's reaction to physical contact from others. For those with an intense dislike of physical contact, it may be most appropriate to allow the wearing of part of the sports kit under the uniform on relevant days. This technique is also useful for those older pupils who may unknowingly offend others in the changing room by parading semi-naked.

Indoor playtimes

Any unexpected change from the normal outdoor play routine may cause pupils to become anxious or distressed. Some pupils, who enjoy the open playground setting, since they are able to withdraw from the majority, may have difficulties with the relatively claustrophobic atmosphere of indoor playtime. Others, who enjoy being able to run up and down or around playground boundaries, may be equally disturbed by the indoor setting.

Schools working inclusively with pupils with ASD acknowledge that playtimes are generally recommended as free times for *all* pupils, which, for those with ASD, may mean time to indulge in their preferred, self-comforting behaviours. Consequently, these schools allow individuals to use empty hall space to run in, or a designated safe, quiet room to withdraw to during indoor playtimes. Whether this is for part or all of a session may depend on individual needs, and the availability of both supervisory staff and physical space.

Early warning of indoor playtime is therefore recommended, along with the use of visual prompts, especially for those pupils using visual timetables. Pupils may also need to be reminded by visual prompts that they may indulge in their preferred behaviours during indoor playtime. This helps to reduce the anxiety and stress caused by not being able to go outside.

Classroom/playground rules

Many individuals have difficulty interpreting both verbal and unwritten social rules. It can be beneficial, therefore, to encourage pupils to produce their own set of playground or classroom rules by interpreting them in their own words. This ensures their optimum co-operation and understanding. General rules may include, for example, 'Be kind to others', and 'Sit on the chairs'; for the individual, these may be more specifically written as 'No kicking' and 'Sit on my chair'. Should difficult situations later arise, or even look to be arising, staff may verbally or visually remind a pupil of his or her own rule as a precautionary measure.

Asking for help

Pupils may have difficulty in asking for help. For those who prefer to withdraw, any interaction, even one resulting in help, may be distressing. Others who tend to make odd approaches, or are aware of being different, or of making repeated mistakes, are equally challenged. Some pupils, who find it difficult to clearly ask for help, may resort to inappropriate, attention-seeking behaviours. Three of the most useful visual prompting techniques to encourage pupils to *appropriately* ask for help are:

- *Hand up.* One of the simplest ways to ask for help is to raise a hand up. Whilst the majority of pupils quickly pick up on this unwritten rule, those with ASD may need to be taught to remain in their seats and put their hand up. One way to do this is to engineer a 'help' situation; for example, provide a pupil with three questions or tasks, two you know he is capable of dealing with on his own, and one more complicated one with which he will need help. Verbally go through the first two to ensure that he knows what to do, and request that he writes down the answers. Then ask him to attempt the third task/ question and to put his hand up if he needs help. It may be necessary to guide him in this action initially. At first, the staff member will need to be extra vigilant of, and immediately responsive to, a pupil's hand being raised. Once individuals have learned that a raised hand elicits help, they can be encouraged to be more realistic in their expectations by gradually being made to wait longer for a response.

- *Help cards.* Some older pupils may benefit from using help cards. These may be an alternative to raising their hands in situations such as the playground, for example; or may act as a tangible reminder of why they originally raised their hands, especially if they have had to wait a length of time for a response. Appropriate wording on the card might include 'Help', '?', or 'Teacher! I need help with...' This latter also provides an opportunity for pupils to complete the sentence in order to communicate their message to staff. Other helping cards can be individually provided as and when necessary, for example, to express confusion, anger, sadness etc. The use of a pupil's own signs and wording will provide him with a better understanding of when to use the cards appropriately.

- *Help pads/boards.* A most actively inclusive working special educational needs co-ordinator (SENCO) I know of provides individuals with a small 'tear off' notepad (often with a front cover depicting the pupils' special interests) on which to write any problems or situations they may need help with. These range from difficulties at break/lunch-times, to situations in class, or problems with homework – anything in fact that the pupils are finding uncomfortable or upsetting. Pupils are taught to tear off and pin their problem onto the SEN staff notice board. This is simply explained to pupils as 'giving the problem away' (for someone else to deal with). Once a staff member has examined and, if necessary, addressed the problem, he or she informs the pupil of the outcome – especially if it involves other pupils. Although pupils sometimes post 'problems' that solve themselves, for example 'David shouted at me'; then the following day, 'We're friends again now', the technique does seem to be extremely effective in quickly dissipating issues of bullying or teasing, and also in addressing particular behavioural/learning difficulties.

CHAPTER 8

Work materials and methods

Some pupils require detailed intervention strategies relating to their work materials and methods, in addition to the more general techniques and adaptations to working conditions addressed so far. The individual provision of such strategies, together with more realistic staff expectations, go a long way towards preventing or reducing pupils' temper tantrums or displays of physical aggression caused by frustration or confusion over the task.

Whilst it is generally recommended that individuals should be assessed on the *quality* and not the quantity of work they produce, it is reasonable for staff to gradually increase their expectations of work output, once a variety of suitable specialist interventions have been consistently applied.

Handwriting

Poor fine motor skills commonly prevent pupils from achieving their best in terms of handwriting. In extreme cases, individuals acutely aware of difficulties may destroy their written work in temper, either openly or, perhaps more disturbingly, in private. Even young primary age individuals may hide ('lose') a subject book containing what they consider to be untidy work or work that has been corrected by the teacher. As detailed in an earlier chapter, this may for some ultimately result in school refusal.

Handwriting difficulties can be addressed in a variety of ways. Depending on the age of the pupil and the degree of difficulty he or she is experiencing, staff need to be selective about which strategies and techniques to adopt. Moreover, having adopted any particular one(s) they may need to teach pupils to generalize these across different subject areas.

• *Letter/word formation.* Individuals may benefit from being encouraged to refine single letter or word formation. This may be done most easily by tracing a finger in sand, either in the classroom sandpit for younger pupils, or, for older ones, in an A4 size sand tray. Alternatively, portable chalk/wipe boards may be used, or if these aren't available, a piece of laminated A4 paper. Whilst all of these methods offer pupils and staff the opportunity to easily erase unacceptable efforts, the use of laminated A4 paper further offers the opportunity for acceptable ones to be photocopied, reduced and pasted into books as tangible, visual prompts and reminders of a pupil's successes. Whilst some schools encourage individuals to use the classroom chalk/wipe board to practise handwriting skills, successful attempts on these are not so easily transferable. However, schools working inclusively with pupils with ASD recognize that acceptable work achieved in this way may be photographed and pasted into workbooks.

• *Writing tools.* Once he or she is confident enough to write directly onto paper or into a book, an individual may display a particular preference for the type of writing tool used (e.g. biro, fountain pen, etc.), or even its colour, in terms of either the ink or the external barrel. Some become so attached to, and reliant upon, the actual writing tool to ensure their 'best' effort they ultimately refuse to even attempt to write without it. If the staff consider that the use of a particular writing tool is fundamental to the handwriting success of the pupil (and this may be verified by looking through earlier written work), then it may be reasonable to ensure the individual always has access to that particular implement. For some, this may mean the provision of several identical items. If the school believes that the wrong writing tools may be contributing to an individual's difficulties, then it is worth spending a few minutes to 'audit' a variety of writing tools to discover a pupil's preference. This may need to be done for those pupils still at the stage of writing with a pencil – some find it easier to use chunkier or shorter pencils; others may prefer, for example, blue pencils rather than the red ones supplied by the school. It is a good idea to equip pupils who use pencils with their own erasers: not only does this allow them to rub out unacceptable attempts, but also significantly reduces any distractions caused by their having to leave their seats to find the shared eraser.

- *Emergent handwriting.* Some pupils benefit from being encouraged to write over yellow felt tip letters/words/numbers. This technique provides pupils with a reasonably discreet formation guide whilst allowing them to complete the task more independently than they otherwise would.

- *Size formation.* For those pupils prone to exceptionally large or small letter/number formation it may be helpful initially to provide enlarged or reduced lined or squared paper to best accommodate the size of their handwriting. Acceptable efforts can later be photocopied to a more usual, legible size and pasted into workbooks. As a pupil becomes more confident in his handwriting efforts, the adapted paper can be gradually reduced or enlarged until it is effectively the same as that in the actual workbooks.

- *Copying from the board.* It is frequently beneficial to provide pupils with a separate piece of paper on which the staff have written the same instructions etc. as those on the board. For those pupils who are easily distracted, this enables greater concentration. For others, who may be particularly slow or reluctant in handwriting, it may make it easier for them to copy the work in a more realistic time. Most pupils are helped by this method, particularly regarding the setting and copying of homework tasks.

- *Computer incentives.* Some pupils may be encouraged to handwrite initially if they are rewarded by being allowed to do alternate words or sentences on the computer. As they participate more willingly, the staff can discreetly increase handwriting expectations (e.g. to two words or sentences) and withdraw the corresponding computer time (e.g. to only one word or sentence).

- *Teacher corrections.* Because individuals may be particularly sensitive to obvious corrections, it may initially be more appropriate to only tick or comment on *acceptable* efforts/passages. Gradually, as a pupil becomes more co-operative, this may be extended to include one or two corrections per page. Particular areas of continued difficulty, such as grammar, punctuation or letter/number formation, can be noted separately, at the back of a book, and addressed at an appropriate time by staff.

Scaffolding

The sheer visual enormity of a complete worksheet may cause some pupils to be reluctant, or even refuse, to begin it. Initially, their anxiety and confusion may be reduced by covering all but the working question with a blank sheet of paper. Some may even need help to write their name in the correct place.

Besides needing help with worksheet tasks, individuals may also require support in creative writing tasks (other associated difficulties are examined in Chapter 9). After initially offering a suggestion for the title, staff may need to suggest a simple beginning sentence, and then encourage the pupil to write it (for some, this may include help with spelling). The pupil should then be encouraged to *tell* another sentence about the original one; he or she should then write this down. The process is repeated with two more sentences about that one, and so on.

Scaffolding provides ample opportunity for staff praise and pupil encouragement, and ensures that a pupil always gets off to the very best start. It may be useful also to provide pupils with a word sheet appropriate for their learning level.

Presentation

Some individuals prefer to present their written work in a column format (that is, quarter of the width of the page). The width of the column can be discreetly increased as the pupil becomes more co-operative. Other individuals prefer a horizontal presentation. One pupil improved 100 per cent in her spelling tests after the staff and her parents encouraged her to learn her words from a horizontally presented list, rather than the more usual vertical list style. This was suggested as a result of noting that, in her workbooks, she often wrote across a double page spread. Once she was provided with workbooks and worksheets with a landscape orientation, her output, quality of work and ability to settle all improved.

Pencil case tools

Even older individuals may benefit from regular supervision and guidance regarding the contents of their pencil case. Whilst supportive parents invariably supply their children with all the necessary equipment, some individuals may misuse tools (e.g. set square for ruler), be reluctant, or ignorant of how, to dispose of worn ones (e.g. empty biros, broken ruler, etc.), or choose to include irrelevant objects for distraction or self-comfort (e.g. pieces of paper to flap, fridge magnets, etc.).

One secondary pupil, who produced good written work with appropriate content, frequently underlined his headings freehand.

Correction by the teacher soon resulted in no underlining at all, which the teacher also had to correct. Headings of *any* sort then disappeared.

Intervention revealed that, although the pupil had his own six inch ruler (the teacher had checked this with him on several occasions), it was broken. The school had previously supplied him with a 12 inch ruler but, because it couldn't fit into his pencil case, he had never thought to use it. The problem was solved once he was provided with a folding 12 inch ruler, and encouraged to use it in each new setting and subject.

CHAPTER 9

Specific subject areas

This chapter examines some common difficulties pupils with ASD have in particular subjects. Together with the next chapter, it draws together other challenges that individuals regularly face. For some pupils, strategies within these chapters may need to be applied in conjunction with those in earlier and subsequent chapters. For others, the strategies included here may be sufficient to address individual difficulties. Whilst this chapter is presented as suitable for all, it has been divided, for ease of reference, into subject area sub-headings.

Literacy

In the previous chapter we examined the difficulties individuals may have with written presentation; now we examine and address those they may have with comprehension, particularly relating to those subject areas in which imagination skills are required (e.g. story writing).

Besides using a scaffolding technique and supporting noun/ verb word sheets etc., some individuals may benefit from drawing a picture of their story subject first. Whilst this is usually the way younger (KS1/2) pupils are initially encouraged to begin story writing, this technique is later dropped in favour of writing only. Allowing older pupils to continue in this way may be beneficial, providing them with a tangible, visual starting point. In some cases, staff may need to provide the drawing or picture; in other cases, telling a pupil to say one sentence about a picture may encourage a story title from which to begin working.

Older pupils, especially those aware of being different, may be reluctant to use this technique unless others within a group are using it as well. In this case it is reasonable to provide a small, sympathetic working group situation, if only once a week. Reward pupil and group efforts by displaying acceptable attempts, to encourage further good work, and also to provide visual reminders of past good efforts.

Because of the combined difficulties individuals face it is unreasonable for staff, especially in the early stages of any story writing, to expect a great output of high quality creative work. Initially eliciting an imaginative story title and one or two short beginning sentences should be seen as sufficient for some. Pupils may not naturally grasp the structure of a story – namely beginning, middle and end. This is most easily encouraged by telling pupils to write one sentence depicting each stage. As pupil confidence, ability and understanding increases, this is then extended to two and three sentences to depict each stage. At the beginning of the process, depending on the pupil's degree of comprehension and other difficulties, one or two words for each stage (e.g. dog standing, dog running, dog asleep) should be seen as acceptable.

Some pupils may benefit from telling alternate sentences to staff to write for them. This is most useful for those pupils who are verbally fluent, but experience difficulties with fine motor skills.

Another useful technique is to use newspaper or magazine reports of a pupil's particular interests. He may then be encouraged to tell, and then write, his own different (or 'smarter') heading, as a good creative starting point.

Individuals, especially those with Asperger syndrome, typically respond well to being asked to do something, or provide an alternative, in a *smarter* or more *intelligent* way. The use of the words *smart* and *intelligent* whenever trying to encourage more appropriate behaviours and responses is therefore very helpful. Even younger pupils respond well to these words, so use them often! For example, when encouraging good walking or sitting techniques, you could say 'Yes, that's one way of doing it, but the really *smart* way of doing it is…'

For some individuals, it is reasonable to suggest a daily or weekly *Smart Target*; for example, Smart Targets are applied to immediately obvious (but not other/educationally detrimental) unwanted behaviours. These may include hanging up of coat, hat etc., and general manners. This will usually be in addition to, and separate from, individual education plan (IEP) targets, although if it transpires to be a real, ongoing need it may, at school discretion, become included in them. Whilst this may indeed be to do with story writing, it may also be applied to other areas of particular need as well. At staff/parent discretion a Smart Target (even if included in an IEP) may be rewarded.

Religious education/history

Many pupils find one or both of these subjects very difficult. The general concept of time, including historical time, is typically challenging for pupils. Using picture story boards to support verbal material is useful, as is setting realistic and achievable working targets. Pupils with good rote memory skills may be encouraged to learn specific dates and events in table or list form.

The national curriculum often includes school visits to different religious or historical buildings and sites. Whilst these may help pupils with ASD to better grasp the reality of subject content, these visits in themselves may also cause a certain degree of anxiety or distress. Early preparation and forewarning of pupils is therefore useful, as is full support (one-to-one if necessary) during a visit. It is further beneficial to liaise with parents beforehand as some pupils may have little or no previous experience of similar family visits. (One family I know of spent months preparing their child for the successful and enjoyable attendance of a family wedding by first showing him videos of other weddings.) In some cases, it may be helpful to provide parents with relevant pictures or cuttings of the place that is to be visited (for example, the outside or inside of churches/libraries etc.), in preparation for school outings.

Physical education/games

Having examined, in Chapter 7, the difficulties that pupils may have with clothes changing for this subject, we now address other challenges individuals may face. For those pupils who prefer to withdraw from others, extra support and encouragement may be required to ensure their full inclusion; this may be by peers or staff, depending on the age of the pupils, and the degree of their difficulty. Other individuals are keen to join in, but prone to making mistakes due to their poor co-ordination. Their support may need to include clear directions on how to join in safely and most appropriately. Some pupils may require specific sequenced prompts for such activities as rope ladder climbing or ball games. (Ball throwing and catching is useful to help improve fine motor skills.)

Specific sequenced prompts differ from three-step prompts in so much as they require a greater number of prompting stages wholly dependent on the activity itself. For rope ladder climbing it may be necessary initially to direct or physically guide each stage of separate hand and foot placement, not only on the ascent but also on the way down. Whilst some pupils with ASD appear to have a natural affinity for climbing (often those also affected with ADHD), others may need to be taught. Those who are able and like to climb may need to be taught safer, more appropriate (smarter/intelligent) ways of doing it, and provided with safer, more appropriate (smarter) places and times *to* do it. For some, often younger, pupils, climbing is a real, although often transient, need. In these cases it is reasonable to include and treat climbing as a self-comforting behaviour. Safe climbing, supervised by staff, may be included in the timetable and used as a reward or incentive.

Any new or challenging PE or games task should be broken into small, easily achievable steps.

Because secondary education often encompasses a much wider variety of physical activities and games than at primary stage, the school cannot reasonably expect a pupil to know how to engage safely in an activity, such as trampolining, without being taught specific rules and methods first. The school may also allow those pupils who may be struggling with certain activities (e.g. long distance cross country running) to complete just part of the course. This then ensures that the pupil experiences a degree of success, and staff may later use this to encourage further participation and inclusion.

It is worth remembering that some pupils may have an intense dislike or very real fear of physical contact with others, including close family members. Contact team games such as rugby, or in some cases even football and netball, may therefore initially cause a high degree of anxiety or distress. One supportive father, in preparation for the first time his son was expected to play secondary school rugby, spent many hours watching TV and video clips with his son, and later took him to local games to better prepare him. The preparation also included practice sessions between father and son in the garden. Gradually, after several patient weeks, one or two of his son's friends were included.

> This approach may be successfully adapted for school, especially early in Year 7. Initially, small safe withdrawal games may be introduced, perhaps with the addition of video clips. Depending on the response of the pupil, staff can then either increase their expectations of the pupil's participation in the sport, or provide more suitable alternative activities.

Individuals may show a real, stubborn preference for the position they are willing to play in team games (e.g. bowler/backstop). It is helpful to encourage them to try other positions, even briefly, by rewarding them with a return to their preferred position immediately afterwards. As their confidence increases (supported by successful RLMB), they may be able to alternate the preferred position with other positions more regularly.

Swimming is another activity that may require special attention by staff. Some pupils may need to be familiarized with the pool, the changing rooms and the instructor, and require preparation for travel to the pool (e.g. by bus), to ensure that it is safe.

Mathematics

Whilst some individuals are able to grasp, and excel in, this subject, others may have difficulty with it generally, or in specific areas (e.g. decimals/tables). Where there are particular areas of difficulty, staff must work to find a way of teaching the topic that is relevant to, and easily understood by, the pupil, and provides the pupil with a reason for wanting to learn. If they are unable to do this, they may need to focus on teaching more relevant, 'real life' areas instead. The following are some examples of strategies that use 'real life' situations to teach mathematical concepts:

- Decimals may have little place in the real life world of an individual, other than when applied to money, or being half (or 0.5) of a favourite tomato sauce sandwich at lunch-time. To make the teaching of decimals as relevant as possible, try to include an individual's particular interests. For example, a PC screen, printer and box may be seen as a 'whole' or 'one' computer system. Each item on its own represents 1/3 or 0.3 of it. (Some pupils, particularly those with semantic pragmatic disorder, may respond better to the word 'complete' as opposed to 'whole'.) Likewise, ten tracks on a favourite CD make up a whole/complete CD, one track is a tenth or 0.1, five tracks a half or 0.5 of it, and so on.

- Wherever possible, use supporting visual tools, such as counters, number rulers, money etc. Older pupils may benefit from visits to the shop, accompanied by staff, buddies or parents.

- When teaching timetables, substitute dots, or tangible items (including sweets), for written or spoken numbers to secure greater pupil interest.

- Tangible or edible items are also a good way of teaching a pupil the concepts of 'less' and 'more' and division, especially as the lesson can progress to include the physical sharing and handing out of portions to others in the class.

- Use a pupil's preferred interests or colours wherever possible.

- Adapt the usual mathematical wordings; for example, instead of 'four times four', say 'four packets of Mars bars, each packet with four Mars bars in'.

- One pupil with Asperger syndrome was able to grasp the complicated concepts of area, multiplication and cost by initially basing all workings on pretend 're-carpeting' (in blue – his favourite colour) of his mum's kitchen. Others may be similarly encouraged to 'tile' supermarket floors, railway stations etc.

For those individuals with good rote memory skills, teach one or two mathematical examples before requesting that they complete the next question/sum in exactly the same way. It may be useful to compile and refer to a list of individual preferences and interests in order so that they may be included when teaching particular mathematical concepts. (NB: Whilst some of these preferences may be constant, others, such as TV characters or foods, may change. It is a good idea, therefore, to regularly update any reference list.)

Art

Some individuals, particularly those who are aware of their fine motor difficulties, may be reluctant to participate in art. Sympathetic encouragement and initial help with setting to task will go a long way to boosting a pupil's confidence and therefore inclusion in this subject. Because some individuals may have a very real dislike of, or obsessive preference for, the texture or smell of certain working materials, it may be necessary to discreetly provide some alternative materials. A pupil may be helped to focus on the task much more quickly if the choice of working materials is limited initially; in some cases it may be necessary to limit all choice, and simply provide the required working materials.

In Chapter 8 we examined typical handwriting problems; difficulties in fine motor skills can also be addressed in art, by encouraging pupils to cut out pictures and compile collages, or thread beads to make simple jewelry.

Personal social education (including toileting and masturbation)

- Lack of personal hygiene may cause great difficulties for some individuals including being teased and bullied. Even some older pupils may be extremely reluctant to regularly clean their teeth, wash and brush their hair, wash their hands, or change their clothes, and become angry or defiant when requested to do so. Early multi-disciplinary intervention, fully supported by,

and agreed with, parents and carers, is the most sensible way of approaching this.

- For optimum results it is best to firmly and consistently approach any personal hygiene task as simply another learning task; that is, break it into small, easily achievable steps, adapt language, and use visual prompts and sequencing etc. as required. Introduce incentives and rewards where appropriate, and as agreed by home and school. Some pupils may require staff support initially in activities such as hand washing, hair brushing, deodorizing etc. at the appropriate times of the school day.

- In all cases, the more often *any* new routine is encouraged, the more familiar it becomes to an individual, thus making it easier and quicker for him or her to understand the importance of it, and to respond most appropriately.

- Schools working inclusively with pupils with ASD will acknowledge the necessity of including any ongoing and obvious personal hygiene problem as an IEP or Smart Target. Many parents of children with ASD experience very real difficulties with their children in this teaching area; it is therefore essential that the school remains sympathetic and supportive as they liaise with the parents in dealing with this problem.

- Some individuals dislike, or are genuinely frightened of, having their hair cut. For girls who are able and willing to tie their hair back, this may not be such a problem; for boys, especially the older ones, it may sometimes be necessary to re-explain the hairstyle or in some cases even to bend the rules a little. One Year 9 male pupil with Asperger syndrome looked set to be detained for having a 'Number 1' crew cut. Whilst written school policy dictated a 'short and tidy' style for boys (there is no denying his was), this was based on the unwritten rule and social understanding that anything shorter than a

'Number 3' cut was deemed a fashion style, therefore unacceptable. In this particular case, 'short and tidy' was redefined more explicitly and with appropriate wording, and there were no further difficulties for the pupil.

- Older pupils, particularly those aware of being different, may benefit from the encouragement of a sympathetic peer or buddy who can support them in their efforts to attain appropriate personal hygiene goals.

- Smearing is an extreme behaviour, unpleasant and upsetting for both the parents and the school. In both the cases I have known, the behaviour was temporary. In each instance, the strategy was to ignore the behaviour in so much as not providing consequences for it. To a young child with autism (both the above-mentioned cases involved children at the KS1 level), it may simply be a matter of discovering another material with which to draw on the walls; alternatively, it may be another behaviour that elicits a great deal of undivided adult attention. As mentioned earlier, it is often far more helpful to focus on positive behaviour, no matter how fleeting.

- A more common toileting difficulty, even with older pupils, is that of the pupil failing to pull up his or her clothes, and emerging from the cubicle half-dressed. This is most easily and sensibly approached by reminding pupils to dress properly *before* coming out, and sending them back *into* the cubicle to do this if they have forgotten. Depending on the age and comprehension level of the pupil, staff and parents may need to be quite specific initially about what is required.

- Many schools have installed electric hand dryers into toilet areas, and whilst some individuals are willing and able to use these, others may be frightened by the noise or feeling of hot air on their hands. In extreme cases this may result in a pupil's refusal to wash his or her hands. In such instances, the school may view it as reasonable to supply paper towels to use instead. Other individuals may need the additional encouragement of using a small hand towel brought from home. (This must be stored away out of sight when not in use.)

- Depending on the general reaction of the class to sex education, particularly at secondary level, it may be more appropriate to provide lessons in small, sympathetic group situations. This may mean, therefore, the temporary withdrawal of some pupils from the class. Specialist teaching materials are available, and can be accessed from (and supported by) SSTs or Specialist School Nurses. Some individuals may be more vulnerable (this can include those with dyspraxia, or other difficulties commonly associated with ASD), and may benefit from a holistic programme of one-to-one education from a variety of specialists.

- Even if it seems that the climate in the classroom is suitable for pupils with ASD, it may still be necessary and beneficial to allocate one-to-one support during sex education. It is helpful in addition to encourage parents and carers to discuss the content of the lesson afterwards, to ensure their child's comprehension of it. In cases where parents or children are reluctant to cross the home/school boundary, it may be more appropriate for school to set aside one-to-one or small group 're-cap'/'understanding' time.

- It may be necessary in some instances for staff to address displays of public masturbation by some individuals. In these cases, staff and parents must work together, and be quite specific about where, when and what is, or is not, publicly permitted. One SENCO, having told a secondary pupil he was 'not allowed to do that in class', found herself the next day having to tell him he was 'not allowed to do that in the playground, either'. Whilst public displays of masturbation in school are obviously not acceptable, it is unreasonable to respond with detention or other such consequences. If, in spite of staff/parent intervention, this behaviour continues, further specialist or even medical intervention may be appropriate. School Nurses or GPs are both useful parties for helping to explain more acceptable times and places for masturbation (e.g. in the bathroom or bedroom, in private at home).

Homework

Whilst homework is not generally viewed as a school 'subject', it may be useful to treat it as such, in order to help individuals with ASD (and their families) deal with it most effectively. Teaching or support staff can best assist in this by spending a few minutes with individuals at the end of any lesson in which homework has been set, to clarify expectations and content. This will often entail using many of the interventions examined in earlier chapters, including help cards.

Whilst some inclusive schools acknowledge the importance of helping pupils with their homework, by providing supported lunch-time working groups, others do not. Experience suggests that individuals generally do want to keep up with homework, but simply do not know how to (or what is actually required), and need a safe and non-threatening environment in which to do it. For those individuals reluctant to cross the home/school boundary, the challenge of doing *home*work (in effect, *school* work) at home is inevitably greater. For those easily prone to distraction, the natural busyness of a thriving family environment may make it difficult to set to task initially, and to maintain concentration. Other pupils who tend to be more withdrawn may not have approached staff for clarification of the expectations before setting to work on their homework, and have similar difficulties in completing it.

There are several ways for school to assist in this. In some cases the staff may need to write out the homework requirements in the pupil's diary. They may also need to help with planning and prioritizing, and write reminders further on in the diary to indicate the date by which homework has to be handed in. Different colour pens are useful for this (e.g. blue for the homework topic, red for the hand-in date). Others may prefer to mark the hand-in date with an asterisk or smiley face reminder.

Longer term homework tasks or projects may need to be broken down into specific weekly targets. I have known cases where inadequately informed pupils have misunderstood the requirements and worked all night, much to the exasperation of their parents, in order to try to complete an entire term's project in one night, over and above other homework also set for that particular evening. I have also known some pupils to ultimately refuse to do any homework at all because of several distressing experiences with it in the past. Such experiences may include whole family arguments and disruption; in fact, this type of disruption due to homework issues is so common that Dr Tony Attwood has suggested that, in extreme cases, certain pupils should be exempt from homework, if agreed by both school and parents (Attwood 2003). Whilst experience suggests that even quite extreme homework difficulties can be managed with specific interventions, there is certainly an argument for decreasing the amount of it, especially during those times when pupils may be experiencing cyclical mood swings (see section in Chapter 1, 'Familiarization techniques specific to secondary school settings').

It may be helpful to supply some pupils with homework folders, which can be colour co-ordinated for different subjects or days of the week. One secondary school set up a very simple homework folder system whereby a pupil was encouraged to collect his folder (with his homework sheet already in it), do that homework the same night, and then return it to school the next morning. Whilst this is a useful way to lay the foundation for good practice in managing homework, particularly with younger pupils, it may need to be viewed more as a first stage intervention for older pupils. Subsequent stages might include, for example, encouraging the pupil to write out, or collect the homework assignment from the teacher before being responsible for placing it in his folder; gradually the number of worksheets or assignments included in the folder can be increased.

Another bonus of using separate homework folders is to make homework more easily accessible and identifiable, not only to students but also to parents.

Earlier, it was recommended that pupils should be assessed on the *quality* and not *quantity* of their work; it therefore seems reasonable to apply this to homework as well. For example, younger pupils might be expected to learn only five instead of ten spelling words. As their confidence increases and they experience success, so also can staff and parents begin to raise their expectations.

Throughout the book mention has been made of the importance of good communication between home and school, and nowhere is this working relationship more important than in the area of homework, if a pupil is to be fully included. Liaison between home and school will be explored more thoroughly in Chapter 12.

Registration

Pupils who have difficulty concentrating, especially younger individuals, may resort to inappropriate self-comforting behaviours during registration. These behaviours may include distracting or disrupting others, wandering across to the computer, etc. It is subsequently more difficult for staff to then focus pupils' attention onto the next task.

Whilst the majority of schools tend to conduct registration by calling surnames alphabetically, more inclusive schools acknowledge the need to adapt this, and call the names of those pupils who are easily distracted sooner rather than later. These individuals can then be set to their next task immediately; tasks such as lining up at the door, writing the date in their books, turning to a certain page in their workbooks, etc. As a pupil's ability to wait patiently for his or her name to be called improves, staff extend the waiting time discreetly until the pupil's name is in the correct place in the register.

Verbally praise a pupil for 'good waiting' to encourage further desirable behaviour.

Individuals may also need to be taught how to respond appropriately to their name when it is called at registration.

CHAPTER 10

Friendship skills

Together with obvious academic challenges, there are also social difficulties facing pupils with autism in the mainstream setting. We have
already examined the value of small groups and other strategies to
help in the academic learning process, whilst avoiding the singling
out of pupils with ASD; now we will explore some strategies specifically related to building the social skills of these pupils. It is generally
recommended and viewed as beneficial to focus primarily on pupil
behaviour, including good sharing and friendship skills, to enable
inclusive academic learning later on.

Some pupils are keen to make friends and join in, and although
each new socializing opportunity is met with enthusiasm, some help
may be required, both in guiding these pupils towards the most
supportive and sympathetic friends, and ensuring that their initial
approaches are socially acceptable. For those pupils who prefer to
withdraw from others, it may be most appropriate to teach social
skills on a one-to-one basis, before introducing one or two sympathetic friends. Nearly all pupils will require some encouragement in
even the most basic of friendship skills.

The skill of sharing

For many pupils, learning to share at school is a skill that may need to
be taught, despite the fact that many will have already learnt how to
share with siblings at home. Depending on the individual, this may

include being taught about sharing physical working space, materials, adult attention, friends, time, etc. With younger pupils, and with older ones in new situations and settings, it is reasonable to expect only a minimal amount of sharing to begin with.

One way to teach about and encourage sharing is to point out to pupils when they are doing it, and reward them appropriately. This is most easily done with the sharing of working materials and space, but may also include the sharing of other people. When 'good sharing' is the focus of the teaching, it should be praised in as many situations and settings as possible.

There are programmes available to help teach sharing and friendship skills, though it is useful initially to prepare pupils for these by doing some individual work with them. Because of their inability to generalize, pupils may need to be taught these skills both in and out of the classroom. In some cases, staff may need to engineer some 'real life' situations whereby the pupils experience a degree of success in their use of sharing and friendship skills.

- *Round games.* These are non-threatening, fun ways of teaching pupils how to share space, time, activity and adult attention. For optimum results it is best to work in a small, manageable group of no more than three or four, supported by sympathetic peers. The verbal sharing of nursery rhymes, important or exciting happenings or particular worries regarding school can all be included in rounds. Depending on individual needs and the age group, other rounds might include suggestions of smart ways to ask for help, and the facial expression and body gesture that should be used when doing so. Some pupils may benefit from being taught how to play board games such as snakes and ladders, draughts, etc. Whilst younger pupils often have games such as these included during activities, this may not be the case for older pupils, who may still benefit from the inclusion of board games, cards and so on to encourage their skills in sharing. These sessions could be held during breaks or lunch-times, or otherwise timetabled in, depending on the availability of staff, and parental agreement. Break and lunch-time sessions might include sharing of outdoor activities and playground apparatus, etc. Once pupils have experienced and understood what good sharing is, and have been taught, in a fun way, how to share, they can be encouraged to adapt and use their knowledge and skills in the classroom.

- *Small group working.* A small group situation of any kind frequently provides an excellent opportunity for staff to teach and encourage physical sharing of working materials, space, etc. Staff may need to perceive the teaching of sharing in the same way they would any other academic learning task, in that it needs to be rewarded with stickers and so on. For some pupils, this may mean temporarily reducing or setting aside other work or behavioural expectations in order to focus fully on good sharing. For others, it may be taught alongside their individual curriculum. In all cases, as a pupil's confidence, and understanding of what is good sharing, increase, so too can the expectations of staff.

- *'Best' friends.* Typically, individuals have difficulty sharing their friends. This may be despite the fact that the chosen 'friend' is in truth reluctant to be a friend at all, and may not be behaving in a friendly manner. Individuals often benefit from being taught exactly what a good friend is and does, not just during play, but also during lessons. Earlier we have mentioned the fact that sometimes individuals need to be guided towards more suitable friendships, if their preferred one is deemed unsuitable. It may also be that the friendship is unhealthy in that the individual is becoming wholly reliant upon it at school. Pupils may need to be taught that it is smart to have more than one friend, and to accept they do not have to be friends with everybody.

General social skills

- *Drama training.* Drama is especially useful for individuals with Asperger syndrome, and particularly recommended by Tony Attwood. It is helpful for speech training, and for teaching body language, social scripts, and acceptable and appropriate social style. Whilst there is some inclusion of these in the Secondary SULP programme (see following bullet point), some individuals may benefit from extra, more focused drama training sessions. These may be video taped, and 'freeze framed' to teach specific skills, such as how to offer and accept constructive criticism, assistance, compliments, sharing, etc. Another useful outcome of drama teaching may be for individuals to learn how to resolve conflict independently and fairly, without the use of expletives or violence, and including the offer of a sincere apology.

- *Specialist programmes.* Programmes to assist an individual in friendship and sharing skills may be accessed from SSTs, who may also support teachers in the delivery of the programme. If a school has a high percentage of SEN pupils, it may consider investing in its own programme. One such programme that is highly recommended is Wendy Rinaldi's *Social Use of Language Programme (SULP)* (Rinaldi 1995). It is available in KS1, KS2 and Secondary formats, and is designed to be run with small groups of four, namely the designated pupil plus one other of similar social need, and two pupils to give support. Experience would suggest that even the supporting pupils benefit from the programme content, with feedback from parents and schools being extremely positive.

At KS1 and KS2 levels, SULP sessions run for 20 to 30 minutes; secondary sessions are approximately one hour. For optimum results, sessions should be once a week for six consecutive weeks. Prior to beginning a SULP programme, the school should arrange a meeting between the parents of the designated pupil and the specialist worker. There should also be a feedback meeting once the programme is finished. The parents of the other pupils involved can be informed by letter of their child's participation in the programme.

Besides teaching skills of friendship and sharing, SULP also focuses on pupils' ability to concentrate, observe and listen, making it a useful tool to help support those with ADHD and other difficulties associated with ASD.

- *Other resources to teach friendship skills.* Whilst there is an extensive array of other useful friendship skills resources available (often accessed via SSTs) initially, other well known and recommended ones include:

    - *Social Stories* (Gray 1994)

    - *My Social Stories Book* (Gray and White 2002)

    - 'Taylor-made' board games
      www.oceansofemotions.com

    - Facial Traffic Lights
      www.oceansofemotions.com

    - The Sims (CD Rom)
      www.thesims.ea.com/index_flash.php

CHAPTER 11

Breaks and lunch-times

Pupils commonly find these naturally noisy and chaotic times difficult to cope with, leading many of them to resort to inappropriate, self-comforting behaviours. The inability of many individuals to generalize and naturally pick up on unwritten social rules and cues may prevent them from joining in most appropriately. Those pupils who prefer to withdraw from others could be allowed some quiet withdrawal time (perhaps in a designated and supervised quiet room), as an incentive or reward for joining in and playing outside. Other pupils, who may be keen to join in and socialize, may first need to be taught how to do this. This might involve staff supervision of their play in a small group situation, or in the playground.

It is helpful to introduce pupils to supervisory staff both in and out of the dining hall. In the case of those pupils who are older, or who are aware of being different, and reluctant to attract attention, these instructions can be supported and guided by peer buddies. Schools working inclusively with pupils with ASD acknowledge the importance of informing midday supervisory assistants (MSAs) of pupils with autism in their care, and providing MSAs with any specialist training and/or information that may be required.

Just as in the classroom, individuals may need to be taught how to use eating tools and play apparatus most appropriately and safely. They may also need to be taught how to ask for help, approach others, wait patiently, line up, sit appropriately, share with others and so on. Some may need to be guided to sit next to sympathetic role models in the dining hall; others may feel safer, or be more easily observed and supervised, if they are within sight of the teachers' table, or supervisory staff. Younger pupils may need to have a chair labelled with their name in the dining hall.

Should individuals have a preference for food of a particular type or colour, serving staff should accommodate this initially by supplying more of the preferred food and less of the other food; gradually they can reduce the amount of the preferred food until it is in line with the majority. Providing parents with the school menu gives them the opportunity to supply a packed lunch for their child on the days that known disliked foods will be served.

Because some dining halls are so noisy and chaotic, pupils tend either to rush through their meal, or refuse to eat their lunch at all, much preferring to be playing outside with others, or withdrawing into a quiet corner. Those individuals who prefer to withdraw, or those who are prone to exceptionally messy eating, may need to be provided with a quiet, screened area to retreat to; this may need to be supervised by staff or buddies, depending on the availability of staff and the degree of difficulty of the situation. As pupils are encouraged and learn how to enjoy meal times more appropriately, they may be returned to the majority.

In extreme cases, some individuals may try to manipulate one-to-one adult attention, or withdrawal time from the dining hall, by displaying wholly inappropriate or disruptive behaviours. Whilst it would *appear* sensible to accommodate this in order to diffuse a situation as quickly as possible, it would also unwittingly set a pattern that would be hard for staff and pupils to break subsequently. It is essential, therefore, that staff remain aware of this possibility before sending a child out of the dining hall, or disciplining him later for his inappropriate behaviour. As mentioned in the introduction, 'inappropriate' behaviour is far more likely to be a pupil's most effective way of communicating his or her real needs and wants.

Occasionally, an individual may complain of hunger or thirst immediately after a break or lunch-time. Experience suggests that such proclaimed hunger or thirst is not only always real, but can also be detrimental to the individual's ability to pay attention to a task. Whilst the provision of a snack or a drink outside of break-times should not become a regular occurrence, staff may initially need to view it as another teaching/learning task, much the same as appropriate toileting. This may include having to remind the pupil to eat or drink before the start of the next session. Initially it may also be necessary to remind the pupils that, having left the classroom during a lesson to have a snack or a drink, they must finish the task they were working on, once they return.

To avoid the possibility of a pupil viewing this temporary provision of a snack during class time as a reward, it is best to provide only water and a very plain biscuit, and withhold as much adult attention (eye contact, conversation, etc.) as possible, during this time.

A further resource to help with breaks and lunch-times: *Including Pupils with Autism at Break and Lunchtimes* (Hewitt 2003).

CHAPTER 12

Reviewing progress

Home/school liaison

The importance and benefits of a good home/school relationship has already been mentioned. Schools working inclusively with pupils with ASD acknowledge this importance and accept responsibility for not only initiating such a liaison, but encouraging it throughout the school life of each pupil. Home/school liaison is essential for parents of children with ASD, but may also be beneficial for parents of other SEN children, especially those with difficulties commonly associated with ASD, such as dyspraxia, whether or not an official diagnosis has been made.

Parent/teacher meetings

A good home/school relationship begins with the introduction of parents to their child's new class teachers and support staff and to the head teacher of the school. It is most beneficial if these introductions take place during the familiarization process.

Whilst formal meetings with parents may appear time consuming, perhaps even nearly impossible, at the beginning of a busy term, experience proves that they are vital if an individual's specific needs are to be met most consistently and appropriately.

Schools working inclusively with pupils with ASD set aside one or two days at the end of term, or the beginning of a new one, to accommodate parent meetings. These might involve, if agreed by the

SENCO and the head teacher, the pupil's designated support staff; certainly, inclusive schools are aware of the importance of making all relevant staff accessible to parents, and providing them with staff names and/or liaison books to enable easier communication. Experience shows that parents are keen to be included and kept regularly informed about their child's progress at school.

Daily liaison books

The daily upkeep of a liaison book is an achievable, affordable way to ensure home/school communication lines are kept open. The most simple format involves the school first recording a success of the day (there will inevitably be at least one, even on what seems to be the worst of days), followed by a difficulty. Because some older pupils may read and be affected by the content of a liaison book, particularly where it concerns areas of difficulty, staff and parents may need to pre-determine a 'communication code'. This may involve using different colour pens for the most urgent issues rather than writing about them in full. Alternatively, a tick or an initial could be written beside something seemingly innocuous to highlight its real importance, and some sort of coding could be used to indicate the need for parents to contact the school urgently, if required.

Depending on their age and ability, individuals may be encouraged to write their own comments about their day, such as one good thing and one bad thing. Alternatively, they might dictate these comments to parents or staff to write for them. This is a good way to begin dealing with particular areas of difficulty. As these difficulties gradually subside, liaison books are used weekly rather than daily, with the ultimate aim of withdrawing them altogether.

Where an individual has a special interest, the liaison book could be covered or decorated with paper or stickers relating to the interest, to make it more personal and familiar.

Another advantage of using liaison books is that less important, though still relevant, issues can be addressed immediately, rather than waiting to include them at more formal review meetings. It is important that any ongoing issues that are being addressed through the liaison book should also be raised during more formal reviews of the individual's programme, such as statement or IEP reviews.

Statement review meetings (SRMs)

Statement review meetings provide good opportunities for more direct home/school liaison. Whenever possible, they should include all the other professionals who are involved, either in person, or in the form of written reports from them. Schools working inclusively with pupils with ASD also acknowledge the importance and benefits of pupil input as well. If the school and parents agree, a pupil may attend all or part of a meeting depending on his or her age and ability. In some cases, it may be more appropriate for the pupil to write a statement or report to be presented at the meeting. In these instances, the staff may need to use a combination of the special interventions previously referred to; these may include: early fore-warning; visibly timetabling in an opportunity to write a report; providing a quiet working area; using a scaffolding question technique; and providing the pupil with incentives and rewards for his or her appropriate participation.

Inclusive schools further acknowledge that, due to pupils having to cope with so many changes and pressures during a whole year period, interim statement review meetings may be required. These may be most simply arranged at the time of the initial annual meetings, and may or may not include the other professionals involved with the individual.

Careers Advice

For all pupils with special educational needs, including those with ASD, the school is further responsible for inviting a Specialist Careers Adviser to attend a 14 Plus Statement review meeting. If appropriate, parents may also attend. Although general health and medical conditions are considered, so also are particular interests, hobbies and aptitudes. As those with autism frequently have special interests and abilities, consideration of these may lead to suitable employment that is both fulfilling and enjoyable, although this may not be in such an obvious way. For example, a pupil with an obsessive interest in car registration plates was eventually happily employed as an operator of a speed camera on a motorway.

It is important that parents and schools focus on the pupils' strengths, and take into consideration their unique and alternative ways of thinking, in order to guide them into the most suitable employment.

Individual education plans (IEPs)

As mentioned in Chapter 9, individual education plans may or may not include a Smart Target – that is, to address an immediately obvious/repetitive unwanted behaviour, although not one detrimental to others or the educational learning process. Depending on individual needs, they may also include less academic targets, such as 'good sharing' or acceptable transition around school. Whatever the target, it is unreasonable for staff to expect a pupil to meet it without having it adequately explained and taught first. For some, this may require using a combination of special interventions such as adapted language, word auditing, sequenced (and/or visual) prompts, etc.

With specialist prompting, older or more able pupils may be able to identify their own starting points from which to reach an ultimate target. For example, a pupil might be instructed to identify one thing he or she finds easy, and one thing he or she finds difficult with writing, and this may help him or her to find a good starting point for reaching the wider literacy target of 'Produce more work'. Likewise, the very wording of targets (e.g. 'Set to task straight away') may need to be audited to give pupils and staff a clearer understanding of what is really required.

Whenever setting any new IEP target, be sure to avoid those that may be obtuse or too general; instead, aim to set specific and easily achievable targets.

> Remember, the ultimate achievement of a target will depend less on the performance of a pupil (who may have little or no understanding of it), and more on the education and encouragement he or she receives from staff and parents.

Therefore, in setting targets, consideration should be given to the availability of staff and other physical resources (e.g. buddy support, etc.). Further consideration should be given to whether or not there are adequate opportunities in the timetable to focus on a set target. It is unreasonable, for example, to expect that a wide target such as 'Appropriate behaviour in PE' could be achieved if the teaching opportunity occurs only once a week, or is not initially supported on a one-to-one basis by staff. Having supported a pupil to reach a specific target, and helped provide him or her with a positive RLMB experience, staff can discreetly increase their expectations of the pupil to be more in line with the majority.

Whilst many schools do not consider the setting of IEPs appropriate or relevant until a few weeks after a new term begins, more inclusive schools should acknowledge the benefits and importance of setting these, in consultation with parents, during the familiarization process. This is especially important when a pupil enters Year 7. As already examined, this is a particularly vulnerable time for many pupils, and one during which, if no plan is instigated, pupils may develop some negative learning patterns and behaviours that are not only hard for staff to correct subsequently, but also distressing for all concerned.

Because of their special knowledge of their child, and previous school experience, many parents strive to arrange that an IEP should be set up for their child before a new term begins, or in the first week of a new term. However, current bureaucracy and educational process does not always easily allow this to happen. It is important that, if a school is to be fully inclusive, then arrangements should be made such that IEPs are set up early in the new term on a much more regular basis.

Key points in the successful mainstream inclusion of pupils with ASD:

- Regular and sympathetic home/school liaison.
- Full consideration of parental experience and specialist knowledge of their child.
- Interim statement review meetings.
- Specific, achievable IEP targets (maximum of three or four).
- New term IEPs included in the familiarization process (especially in Year 7).
- Flexibility, and consideration of the unique and alternative thinking of someone with ASD when planning career choices.

Afterword

Before I leave you, filling with guilt

Maybe you could think before you next jilt

The boy who only wanted to be treated the same

If that doesn't happen, who is to blame?

From *The People to Blame* by Christopher Ogden (aged 13)

Christopher, thank you. You are an excellent poet.

References

Asperger, H. (1994) 'Autistic Psychopathy in Childhood.' In U. Frith (ed.) (1997) *Autism and Asperger Syndrome.* Cambridge: Cambridge University Press.

Attwood, T. (2003) 'Frameworks for Behavioural Interventions.' *Childhood and Adolescent Psychiatric Clinics of North America 12,* 1, 65–86
www.tonyattwood.com.au

Gray, C. (1994) *Social Stories.* Arlington, TX: Future Horizons.
www.futurehorizons-autism.com

Gray, C. and White, A.L. (2002) *My Social Stories Book.* London: Jessica Kingsley Publishers.

Hewitt, S. (2003) *Including Pupils with Autism at Break and Lunchtimes.* Tamworth: Nasen.

Kanner, L. (1943) 'Autistic disturbances of affective contact.' *Nervous Child 2,* 217–50.

Rinaldi, W. (1995) *The Social Use of Language Programme (Primary and Pre-School Teaching Pack).* Windsor: NFER-NELSON.

Wing, L. and Gould, J. (1979) 'Severe impairments of social interaction and associated abnormalities in children: Epidemiology and classification.' *Journal of Autism and Developmental Disorders 9,* 11–29.

References

Index